W9-CGO-995

Tina Smith

MORE
MAKE-A-MIX
COOKERY

by Karine Eliason, Nevada Harward & Madeline Westover

Cover Photo: Clockwise from left: SWEET QUICK BREAD MIX, page 11, Slice and Bake Sugar Cookies, page 42, GRANOLA MIX, page 24, WHOLE-WHEAT HOT ROLL MIX, page 33, ITALIAN-STYLE MEAT MIX, page 38, COOL CARROTS MIX, page 29, and FIVE-WAY BEEF MIX, page 42.

Contents

ANOTHER BEST-SELLING VOLUME FROM HPBooks®

Publisher: Rick Bailey
Editorial Director: Retha M. Davis
Editor: Carroll P. Latham
Art Director: Don Burton
Book Design: Tom Jakeway; Book Assembly: Ken Heiden
Book Manufacture: Anthony B. Narducci
Typography: Cindy Coatsworth, Joanne Nociti, Patty Thompson
Food Stylist: Janet Pittman
Photography: George de Gennaro Studios

Notice: The information contained in this book is true and complete to the best of our knowledge. All recommendations are made without any guarantees on the part of the author or HPBooks. The author and publisher disclaim all liability in connection with the use of this information.

Published by HPBooks, Inc., P.O. Box 5367, Tucson, AZ 85703   602/888-2150
ISBN: 0-89586-055-4 Library of Congress Catalog Card No. 80-82533
©1980 HPBooks, Inc. Printed in U.S.A.
2nd Printing

Cover Photo: Clockwise from left: SWEET QUICK BREAD MIX, page 11, Slice and Bake Sugar Cookies, page 42, GRANOLA MIX, page 24, WHOLE-WHEAT HOT ROLL MIX, page 33, ITALIAN-STYLE MEAT MIX, page 38, COOL CARROTS MIX, page 29, and FIVE-WAY BEEF MIX, page 42.

Karine Eliason, Madeline Westover & Nevada Harward

When you are convinced you have the answer to a problem shared by millions of people, you want to share your knowledge. This is what Karine Eliason, Madeline Westover and Nevada Harward have been doing since before the publication of their first book, *Make-a-Mix Cookery*.

With the great success of *Make-a-Mix Cookery*, the authors were inspired to create more mixes to share. Many people have written asking for additional ideas for mixes and have shared mixes they prepare. There was an apparent need for additional mixes which stored well for long periods of time—resulting in their refrigerator and freezer mixes. Many requested small quantity mixes for one or two people while others asked for mixes containing whole-wheat and little or no preservatives.

They have been praising the joys of using mixes as they lecture extensively throughout the United States, appearing on TV and demonstrating before large groups. Wherever they go they are recognized as the *mix ladies* and are asked to give impromptu demonstrations.

Karine, Madeline and Nevada all do volunteer work in youth and women's organizations. With their busy schedule and large families—they have 18 children among them—they get everyone involved. Older children learn to make mixes and prepare meals while the younger children learn to make simple main dishes and desserts from mixes. The mix ladies also use mixes while on vacations with their families. They find mixes an economical and efficient way to eat well with little preparation or clean-up while on the road.

Mixes Are Universal

Everyone who cooks uses mixes. Did you ever prepare a casserole ahead of time? An extra large batch of cookies? Plan how you'll use leftovers from Sunday's roast beef? If you did, you used the philosophy behind mixes. You prepared foods when it was convenient and used them at a later time.

Commercial mixes are costly and are often laced with preservatives. By comparison, the advantages of homemade mixes are easily recognized. The cost is clearly less for those mixtures you combine in your own kitchen. You know without doubt ingredients you combine are fresh, of high quality and free from most preservatives.

Few commercial mixes meet the needs of small families or those who prefer whole grains, reduced sugar content, little or no salt and no preservatives. We have developed mixes and recipes for these two special-needs groups.

It is our purpose to aid you, no matter what your special needs, to develop the art of preparing low-cost, nutritious and attractive meals in less time through the use of homemade mixes.

What Is A Mix?

A mix combines basic ingredients that can be stored for future use. As we developed mixes, we expanded that definition. Our mixes also:
1. Cut down meal preparation time.
2. Cost less than commercial mixes.
3. Are nutritious.
4. Have superior flavor.
5. Contain few or no preservatives.

Mixes can be stored in pantries, refrigerators or freezers. With the exception of mixes for children, you'll find all mix recipes under those classifications. Pantry mixes can be stored in the refrigerator or freezer if you feel you will not use them in the specified time. Some refrigerator mixes can be stored in the freezer. By storing mixes at a colder temperature, storage time is often doubled.

Pantry Mixes, pages 8 to 26, are stored on pantry shelves and generally replace commercially prepared mixes.

Refrigerator Mixes, pages 27 to 35, have a relatively short shelf life. Store these mixes in small quantities unless you have space in your refrigerator for large containers.

Freezer Mixes, pages 36 to 50, include most of our main dish mixes. Plan your menus so they can be properly thawed before using them.

Basic Ingredients

Use only fresh, high-quality ingredients. Become acquainted with store-brand and generic labeled food items to determine their quality before using them in your mixes. Your finished product will only be as good as your ingredients.

All-purpose flour is called for in most of our mixes. If you prefer whole-wheat flour or unbleached flour, see *High Health Pantry Mixes*, pages 24 to 26, and *High Health Refrigerator Mixes*, pages 33 and 35 and *High Health Freezer Mixes*, pages 49 and 50. For recipes, see *High Health*, pages 139 to 148.

We recommend using hydrogenated vegetable shortening in pantry mixes for tender, flaky texture and crisp outer crusts. Shortening can be stored at room temperature for considerable time without turning rancid. Because it holds air pockets in the mixture, the resulting product is larger in volume.

Instant dry nonfat milk powder is used in many of the mixes. Milk adds nutrition and results in a more tender product with good browning qualities. When dry milk powder is used in a mix, you need to add only water. However, fresh milk or dry milk to which water has been added may also be used.

Buttermilk makes light, tender baked goods. It mixes well with other ingredients and adds acid which reacts with baking soda or baking powder to leaven bread products. If your supermarket doesn't carry dry buttermilk powder, ask the manager to do so. It is less expensive than liquid buttermilk and can be added to dry ingredients whenever buttermilk is called for. There is no need to reconstitute it so there is no waste.

Sugar not only adds sweetness, but tenderness to baked products. When a recipe calls for brown sugar, eliminate lumps by pressing the sugar through a coarse sieve. We have reduced sugar to a minimum, especially in the High Health section, pages 139 to 148.

Leavening agents and spices loose freshness rapidly. If your baking powder is flat or spices are weak, don't use them in mixes. It will be better to buy fresh baking powder or cinnamon than to be sorry later when the flavor is not what you expected or a cake doesn't rise as it should.

Meal Planning Magic

Does the challenge of preparing three meals a day, seven days a week, 52 weeks a year boggle your mind? That's over a thousand meals a year! With adequate planning and preparation of mixes, the challenge can become a rewarding experience.

Take time to plan your menus at least one week in advance. One month is better. Then do your major grocery shopping every two to four weeks. Buy fresh produce and dairy products every week. You'll not only know what you're going to fix for dinner each night, but save money. Once you master planning around mixes, you'll prepare delicious, well-balanced meals with little effort.

Start by getting a calendar with squares large enough to write down menus. At first, write down whole meals, then as you get used to planning, write down only the main course. See the menu suggestions on pages 6 and 7.

Keep your family's schedule in mind. If you have a meeting every Wednesday afternoon, plan something requiring little preparation on Wednesday nights. Thursday evening classes will require speedy clean-up. When you'll be away during mealtime and there are children to feed, plan something they can prepare for themselves or a babysitter can prepare with little effort.

Remember, variety is the spice of life. Meals planned around the same meat five nights in a row are monotonous. Alternate using beef, pork, poultry, fish, cheese and egg dishes. You'll find recipes for each of these in *Casseroles & Supper Dishes*, pages 73 to 90, and *Meats, Fish & Poultry*, pages 91 to 99. Plan interesting color and texture combinations. Uninteresting one-color or one-texture meals will give you two things: poor appetites and leftovers.

Generally, large packages of food cost less per serving than small packages. If you prepare meals for one or two people, when your Monday casserole calls for corn, plan to use the rest of the can or package in corn chowder on Wednesday. When you use part of a can of tuna in a salad, use the rest in sandwiches the next day.

Make a list before going grocery shopping, then buy only what you list, unless a lower priced item can be substituted. Check each mix recipe and menu recipe for ingredients needed. When you plan menus calling for a perishable food such as fresh mushrooms, schedule it shortly after your weekly shopping trip. Consider using a single meat for more than one meal but never two days in a row. And last but not least, never shop when you're hungry—it leads to impulse buying.

Store foods properly. Keep canned goods in a cool, dry and dark storage area. Store spices away from the heat of your stove. Pour flour and other similar foods into containers with tight-fitting lids. Refrigerate fruits and vegetables. You may want to keep an extra refrigerator in your service room or garage as we do. This allows us the extra space to store salads, refrigerator mixes, vegetables and fruits.

Preparing Mixes

After shopping, you're ready to begin preparing mixes. Select one day a week or two days a month when you can spend a large part of the day in the kitchen. Working people may want to use Saturdays or evenings. Make out a schedule for each week of the month listing mixes to be made that week. See the three mix sections for specific information on preparing pantry, refrigerator and freezer mixes.

For help in planning menus, see *Sample Menus for One Month*, pages 6 and 7. Recipes prepared from mixes are marked with an asterisk*. You'll find page numbers for recipes in the index. Refer to the recipe for the mix used. Mixes needed to prepare each week's menus are listed with the menus. Remember, this is only a guide. Change the menus to fit your families preferences.

Some mixes take only a few minutes to prepare, while others take time to cut in shortening, combine wet and dry ingredients or cook meat. You can easily dove-tail the preparation of several mixes. For instance, while the meat for ALL-PURPOSE GROUND BEEF MIX, page 37, is cooking, you can prepare several easy mixes such as WHOLE-WHEAT HOT ROLL MIX, page 33, SNACK CAKE MIX, page 11, and CHEF'S SALAD DRESSING MIX, page 28. These three mixes each take about five minutes to prepare. Next, chop onions, green pepper and celery to add to the meat. The meat and vegetable mixture will simmer about ten minutes. That is long enough to prepare CRISP COATING MIX, page 19, and get the ingredients together for SLICE & BAKE SUGAR COOKIES, page 42. While the meat mixture cools, finish making the cookie dough and make WHITE SAUCE BUTTER-BALLS, page 40, FREEZER CHEESE SAUCE MIX, page 36, and CHOCOLATE SYRUP MIX, page 27. Now you are ready to use the menus listed for Week 1 in *Sample Menus for One Month*, pages 6 and 7. These mixes will be used again in the following weeks.

On the same day we make our mixes, since we have already accumulated some clutter, we grate cheese, chop onions and form hamburger patties. These are refrigerated or frozen in recipe-size portions. We also find it helpful to cut carrot and celery sticks, cover them with ice water and store them in the refrigerator to use with meals or for snacking. We like to prepare salads ahead by combining chopped green onions, celery, carrots, cauliflowerets, radishes, broccoli flowerets and leafy greens. Store them in a container with a tight-fitting lid. Because tomatoes and cucumbers cause wilting, add them just before serving. Serve this crisp salad during the week with an assortment of homemade salad dressings.

Storing Mixes

Mixes can be stored in a single large container with a tight-fitting lid or in individual recipe size containers. As you plan your menus, decide how you will store your mixes. You will save time and effort when making a snack cake if the mix is pre-measured and packaged in individual containers.

Mixes that are made of all dry ingredients have a tendency to settle with heavier ingredients on the bottom. Mixes stored in large containers must be stirred before using. Individual packages eliminate this problem. Those mixes containing shortening, such as QUICK MIX, page 21, or SOPAIPILLA MIX, page 9, do not require stirring. Because they are used in varying amounts, they can easily be stored in large containers.

It is important to store pantry mixes in a cool, dry and dark place. Heat, moisture and light destroy freshness. You must use airtight containers, especially if you live in a humid climate.

As you prepare a variety of mixes, it becomes imperative that you know which ones are which. Label each container with the name of the mix and the date by which it should be used. Use the mix within the time specified in the recipe for maximum nutrition and flavor.

When you finish making and storing the mixes, jot down on your calendar when to take out a mix to thaw, make a gelatin salad or do other last-minute preparations.

We hope you find these suggestions helpful and can put them to use in your home. The more you practice meal planning techniques, the easier it becomes and the more liberated you become from your kitchen. Good luck and good planning!

Sample Inventory

Keep a complete inventory of the mixes you make, subtracting packages or cups of mix as they are used. Post the record in a convenient place close to where mixes are stored. You may want three lists for the three types of mixes or one master list. The chart below is simple, easy to keep and if kept up-to-date tells you exactly what you have on hand.

Type	Mix or Food	Expiration Date	No. Pkgs. or Cups	Pkgs. or Cups Used
Pantry	Onion S. Mix	March 20	8 pkgs.	III
	Quick Mix	April 1	7 cups	III
	Snack Cake Mix	April 8	6 pkgs.	II
Refrigerator	WW Hot Roll Mix	March 20	18 cups	LHT I
	Marinade Blend	Feb 10	3 cups	I
Freezer	White Sauce B.B.	April 1	28 pkgs.	LHT II
	Gr. Beef Mix	April 10	6 pkgs.	III
	Sugar Cookies	April 10	4 pkgs.	II

Sample Menus for One Month

Mixes needed to prepare menus:

Week 1
WHITE SAUCE BUTTER-BALLS
CHEF'S SALAD DRESSING MIX
FREEZER CHEESE SAUCE MIX
ALL-PURPOSE GROUND BEEF MIX
SLICE & BAKE SUGAR COOKIES
CRISP COATING MIX
WHOLE-WHEAT HOT ROLL MIX
CHOCOLATE SYRUP MIX
SNACK CAKE MIX

Week 2
MARINADE BLEND MIX
MARY'S ITALIAN DRESSING MIX
QUICK MIX
VANILLA PUDDING & PIE FILLING MIX
SOPAIPILLA MIX
CUBED PORK MIX
BUTTERMILK & ONION DRESSING MIX
CHILI BEANS & WHEAT MIX
SLICE & BAKE CHOCOLATE CHIP COOKIES
GRANOLA MIX

Week 3
MOLASSES & BRAN MUFFIN MIX
GRAHAM CRACKER CRUST MIX
SOUR CREAM & CHEESE MIX
FREEZER PIE CRUST MIX
COOL CARROTS MIX
PRISCILLA'S SALAD DRESSING MIX
CRUMB CAKE MIX
CREAM CHEESE PASTRY MIX
TORTILLA MIX

Week 4
ONION SEASONING MIX
ITALIAN-STYLE MEAT MIX
SLICE & BAKE CHOCOLATE WAFER COOKIES
MEAT LOAF MIX
CHOCOLATE WAFER PIE CRUST MIX

Week 1 Menus

Sunday
Wrapped Chicken Breasts*
Broccoli
Tossed Green Salad with
Chef 's Salad Dressing Mix*
Hard Rolls
Sherbet

Monday
English Poached Eggs & Ham*
Cherry Tomatoes
Stuffed Celery Rounds
Gingerbread

Tuesday
Quick Chow Mein*
Rice
Fruit-Gelatin Salad
Sugar Cookies*

Wednesday
Crunchy Fish Bake*
Green Beans Amandine
Tossed Green Salad
Blue Cheese Dressing*
Fresh Fruit Tray

Thursday
Football Hero Bun*
Football Hero*
Sliced Tomatoes
Carrot Curls
Chocolate Chip Ice Cream*

Friday
Macaroni & Cheese
Carrot & Celery Sticks
Fruit Cup
Applesauce Snack Cake*

Saturday
Pocket Bread*
Avocado Slices
Alfalfa Sprouts
Mushroom Slices
Chopped Tomatoes or Lettuce
Cubed Cheese, Ham or Chicken
Baked Apple

Week 2 Menus:

Sunday
Marinated Flank Steak*
Tossed Green Salad
Mary's Italian Dressing*
Fruit Muffins*
Layered Cream*

Monday
Navajo Tostadas*
Melon slices
Sugar Cookies*

Tuesday
Sweet & Sour Pork*
Rice
Relish Plate
Ice Cream
Quick Fudge Sauce*
Fortune Cookies

Wednesday
Tuna Salad
Buttermilk & Onion Dressing*
Thin Wheat Crackers*
Carrot Snack Cake*

Thursday
Quick Baked Chimichangas*
Shredded Lettuce
Sour Cream
Avocado Slices
Orange Sherbet
Chocolate Chip Cookies*

Friday
Hearty Beef Chowder*
Salty Butter Sticks*
Granola Fruit Crisp*

Saturday
Cheese Pizza
Coleslaw
Buttermilk & Onion Dressing*
Apple Slices

Week 3 Menus:

Sunday
Ham with Cherry Sauce
Glorified Baked Potatoes*
Vegetable-Gelatin Salad
Bran-Ana Muffins*
Lemon Light Dessert*

Monday
Company Casserole*
Marinated Carrot Salad*
Sour Cream & Raisin Pie*

Tuesday
Ham & Potato Casserole
Spinach Salad
Priscilla's Salad Dressing*
Boston Cream Pie*

Wednesday
Chili Tostadas*
Chopped Lettuce
Chopped Tomatoes
Shredded Cheese
Lime Tarts Supreme*

Thursday
Crunchy-Crust Chicken*
Marinated Bean Salad*
Corn-on-the-Cob
Party Trifle*

Friday
Cheese Crisps*
Chopped Lettuce
Chopped Onion
Chopped Tomatoes
Refried Beans
Chocolate Ice Cream Sodas*
Chocolate Chip Cookies*

Saturday
Easy Beef Stroganoff*
Buttered Noodles
Fresh Peas & Onions
Tossed Green Salad
Thousand Island Dressing*
Sliced Bananas, Peaches & Pears

Week 4 Menus:

Sunday
Company Beef Brisket*
Baked Potatoes
Tangy Cauliflower*
Fresh Strawberry Pie

Monday
Eggplant Parmesan*
French Bread*
Creamy Vanilla Pudding*
Chocolate Wafer Cookies*

Tuesday
French Dip Sandwiches
Cole Slaw
Baked Beans or Cowboy Beans*
Chef's Salad Dressing Mix*
Peach Cobbler

Wednesday
Casserole Pizza*
Relish Plate
Ice Cream Sundae Pie*

Thursday
Hurry-Up Curry*
Sliced Cucumbers
Chutney
Sliced Tomatoes
Pineapple-Mint Dessert*

Friday
Cathy's Meatball Sandwiches*
Tossed Green Salad
Priscilla's Salad Dressing*
Baked Custard
Butterscotch Sauce

Saturday
Spanish Cheese Pie*
Italian-Style Zucchini*
Relish Plate
Hard Rolls
Fresh Fruit Plate

* See recipe in index

Pantry Mixes

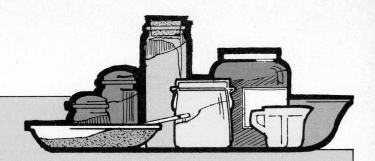

Use equipment already in your kitchen to make pantry mixes. Three items we consider essential are a large round-bottom bowl, a wire whisk and a pastry blender. Electric hand mixers or heavy-duty mixers will save time and labor, but are not essential.

Have your storage materials on hand before you start. Use heavy-duty foil rather than two layers of lightweight foil. It is stronger and less likely to tear or allow moisture to collect. If you prefer plastic bags, use moisture-vapor-proof freezer bags, not thin sandwich bags. Have labels or masking tape and marking pencils or pens ready to label each package or canister.

All ingredients should be free of lumps. Sift powdered sugar, cocoa powder and baking soda. Press brown sugar through a coarse sieve to remove lumps. Use a wire whisk to stir dry ingredients. If baking soda or baking powder is added, stir them at least one minute.

Shortening cut into mixes keeps heavier ingredients from settling to the bottom. Mixes containing no shortening require stirring before they are used. Cut in shortening with a pastry blender or use your mixer if the bowl you are using has a cover. See page 20 for instructions on making your own bowl cover.

This section is divided into three parts: Basic Pantry Mixes, Small Family Pantry Mixes and High Health Pantry Mixes. Consider using all mixes. Some basic mixes are small enough for one or two people; others meet the needs of those concerned with high health. Mixes for small families can be increased for use by a larger family. All of the recipes in the high-health section are suitable for any audience.

TRAIL MIX, HOT COCOA MIX and SPICE BLEND MIX are the only mixes not called for in a recipe. Use up to 2-1/2 teaspoons SPICE BLEND MIX to flavor whipped cream, cake batters, muffin batters, yogurt, pancakes, quick-bread batters, puddings, fruits and custards. You may prefer to start with about 1 teaspoon, then increase the amount until the flavor is acceptable.

Basic Pantry Mixes

Buttermilk Pancake & Waffle Mix

Buttermilk powder is available in most supermarkets.

2 cups dry buttermilk powder
8 cups all-purpose flour
1/2 cup granulated sugar

8 teaspoons baking powder
4 teaspoons baking soda
2 teaspoons salt

In a large bowl, combine all ingredients. Stir with a wire whisk until evenly distributed. Pour into a 12-cup container with a tight-fitting lid. Seal container. Label with date and contents. Store in a cool dry place. Use within 6 months. Makes about 10-1/2 cups BUTTERMILK PANCAKE & WAFFLE MIX.

BUTTERMILK PANCAKE & WAFFLE MIX makes:

Aebleskivers, page 109
Buttermilk Pancakes, page 111

Buttermilk Waffles, page 111

Sopaipilla Mix

If you use a large flat bowl, it is easy to cut the shortening in with a pastry blender.

7 cups all-purpose flour
4 tablespoons granulated sugar
8 teaspoons baking powder

4 teaspoons salt
1/4 cup vegetable shortening

In a large bowl, combine flour, sugar, baking powder and salt. Stir with a wire whisk until blended. Use a pastry blender, a heavy-duty mixer with a bowl cover or your fingers to blend in shortening until evenly distributed. Spoon into an 8-cup container with a tight-fitting lid. Seal container. Label with date and contents. Store in a cool dry place. Use within 10 to 12 weeks. Makes about 8 cups SOPAIPILLA MIX.

SOPAIPILLA MIX makes:
Navajo Tostadas, page 83
Salty Butter Sticks, page 51

Sopaipillas, page 101

Tortilla Mix

You'll enjoy the superior flavor of the tortillas made from this mix.

8 cups all-purpose flour
2 tablespoons salt

1 tablespoon baking powder
1-1/4 cups vegetable shortening

In a large bowl, combine flour, salt and baking powder. Stir with a wire whisk until blended. Use a pastry blender, a heavy-duty mixer with a bowl cover or your fingers to blend in shortening until mixture resembles cornmeal. Spoon into a 10-cup container with a tight-fitting lid. Seal container. Label with date and contents. Store in a cool dry place. Use within 10 to 12 weeks. Makes about 10 cups TORTILLA MIX.

Flour Tortillas

2-1/2 cups TORTILLA MIX, see above
1/2 cup fresh milk

Vegetable shortening

In a medium bowl, combine TORTILLA MIX and milk. Stir with a fork until mixture forms a ball. Turn out onto a lightly floured surface. Knead about 15 times until dough becomes smooth. Divide dough into 10 balls. Grease your hands lightly with shortening. Roll balls of dough in your hands, coating each ball with shortening. On a lightly floured surface, roll out balls to 9-inch circles. Preheat a griddle or a large skillet to 365°F (185°C). Bake tortillas on hot ungreased griddle or skillet about 15 seconds on one side or until bubbles form. Press bubbles down with spatula. Turn tortilla; cook 10 to 15 seconds longer. Remove from pan. Place on a cloth towel. Cover; keep warm. Makes 10 tortillas.

Flour Tortillas make:
Cheese Crisps, page 54
Cheese Tortilla Stacks, page 57

Cinnamon Crispies, page 54

Buttermilk Cookie Mix

Cookies made with this mix are soft and cake-like.

9 cups all-purpose flour
3/4 cup dry buttermilk powder
4 cups granulated sugar
2 teaspoons baking soda

2 teaspoons salt
1-1/2 teaspoons cream of tartar
2 cups vegetable shortening

In a large bowl, stir flour, buttermilk powder, sugar, baking soda, salt and cream of tartar with a large wire whisk until blended. Use a pastry blender, a heavy-duty mixer with a bowl cover or your fingers to blend in shortening until evenly distributed. Spoon into a 16-cup container with a tight-fitting lid. Seal container. Label with date and contents. Store in a cool dry place. Use within 10 to 12 weeks. Makes about 15 cups BUTTERMILK COOKIE MIX.

BUTTERMILK COOKIE MIX makes:

Carrot Cookies, page 129
Cinnamon Jumbos, page 129

Chocolate Cream Cakes, page 128

How to Make Buttermilk Cookie Mix

1/In a large bowl, stir dry ingredients with a wire whisk until evenly distributed.

2/Use a pastry blender to cut shortening into dry ingredients until mixture resembles cornmeal.

Snack Cake Mix

One package SNACK CAKE MIX will make any of the cakes listed below.

8 cups all-purpose flour   **1 tablespoon salt**
2 tablespoons baking soda   **6 cups granulated sugar**

In a large bowl, combine all ingredients. Stir with a wire whisk until blended. Divide mixture evenly into six 2-1/2-cup containers with tight-fitting lids, about 2-1/4 cups each. Seal containers. Label with date and contents. Store in a cool dry place. Use within 10 to 12 weeks. Makes 6 packages or about 13-1/2 cups SNACK CAKE MIX.

SNACK CAKE MIX makes:
Applesauce Snack Cake, page 116   Double Chocolate Snack Cake, page 112
Banana-Walnut Snack Cake, page 116   Oatmeal Spice Cake, page 113
Carrot Snack Cake, page 113

Sweet Quick Bread Mix   *Photo on cover.*

Brown sugar is always packed into the cup to insure a full measure.

6 cups all-purpose flour   **1-1/2 cups granulated sugar**
1 tablespoon baking powder   **1-1/2 cups packed brown sugar**
1 tablespoon baking soda   **1-1/2 cups vegetable shortening**
1-1/2 teaspoons salt

In a large bowl, stir flour, baking powder, baking soda, salt, granulated sugar and brown sugar with a large wire whisk until blended. Use a pastry blender, a heavy-duty mixer with a bowl cover or your fingers to blend in shortening until evenly distributed. Spoon into a 12-cup container with a tight-fitting lid. Seal container. Label with date and contents. Store in a cool dry place. Use within 10 to 12 weeks. Makes about 11 cups SWEET QUICK BREAD MIX.

SWEET QUICK BREAD MIX makes:
Banana-Nut Bread, page 108   Pumpkin Bread, page 110
Carrot-Orange Loaf, page 108   Spicy Applesauce Bread, page 106
Cranberry Bread, page 111   Zucchini Bread, page 110
Date-Nut Bread, page 108

If your container doesn't have a tight-fitting lid, make one with heavy-duty foil. Use tape or an elastic or rubber band to hold the foil in place.

Vanilla Pudding & Pie Filling Mix

Vanilla is added when the mix is made into desserts.

2-1/3 cups granulated sugar
1-3/4 cups cornstarch

3/4 teaspoon salt

In a large bowl, combine all ingredients. Stir with a wire whisk until blended. Pour into a 4-cup container with a tight-fitting lid. Seal container. Label with date and contents. Store in a cool dry place. Use within 4 months. Makes about 4 cups VANILLA PUDDING & PIE FILLING MIX.

VANILLA PUDDING & PIE FILLING MIX makes:
Boston Cream Pie, page 114
Creamy Vanilla Pudding, page 126
Layered Chocolate & Vanilla Dessert,
  page 122

Layered Vanilla Cream, page 122
Sour Cream & Raisin Pie, page 117
Vanilla Cream Pie, page 121

Buttercream Frosting Mix

If you substitute butter or margarine for the shortening, refrigerate or freeze the mix.

10 cups powdered sugar
3/4 cup vegetable shortening

Sift powdered sugar into a large bowl. Use a pastry blender or your fingers to blend in shortening until evenly distributed. Mixture will look like cornmeal. Spoon into a 10-cup container with a tight-fitting lid. Seal container. Label with date and contents. Store in a cool dry place. Use within 6 months. Makes about 10 cups BUTTERCREAM FROSTING MIX.

Vanilla Buttercream Frosting

3 cups BUTTERCREAM FROSTING MIX,
  see above
3 tablespoons butter or margarine, softened

About 3 tablespoons fresh milk
1 teaspoon vanilla extract

In a medium bowl, combine BUTTERCREAM FROSTING MIX, butter or margarine, milk and vanilla. Beat until smooth and creamy. Add additional milk, if necessary. Makes enough frosting for one 8- or 9-inch layer cake.

Variations

Chocolate Buttercream Frosting: Stir 1/2 cup unsweetened cocoa powder into frosting mix before adding butter or margarine. Increase milk to about 4 tablespoons.

Add 1 cup instant nonfat milk powder when making mix. Substitute 3 tablespoons water for milk.

Lemon Pound Cake, page 135, with NUTRI-NUT CEREAL MIX, page 25, SPICED OATMEAL MIX, page 25, CORN BREAD MIX, page 23, HOT COCOA MIX, page 23, CRUMB CAKE MIX, page 23. ONION SEASONING MIX, page 19, is in small container.

Chocolate Wafer Crust Mix

Make the cookies for this mix from SLICE & BAKE CHOCOLATE WAFER COOKIES, page 45.

About 160 2-1/4-inch chocolate wafer cookies
1/2 cup granulated sugar

Break 8 or 10 cookies into blender. Process to make fine crumbs. Pour crumbs into a large bowl. Repeat with remaining cookies to make 8 cups crumbs. Or use a rolling pin to crush cookies between 2 sheets of waxed paper or in a plastic bag. Stir in sugar. Pour into a 10-cup container with a tight-fitting lid. Seal container. Label with date and contents. Store in a cool dry place. Use within 6 months. Makes about 8-1/2 cups CHOCOLATE WAFER CRUST MIX.

CHOCOLATE WAFER CRUST MIX makes:

How to Make Chocolate Wafer Crumbs

1/Break 8 or 10 cookies into blender. Process to make fine crumbs.

2/Or use a rolling pin to crush cookies between waxed paper or in a plastic bag.

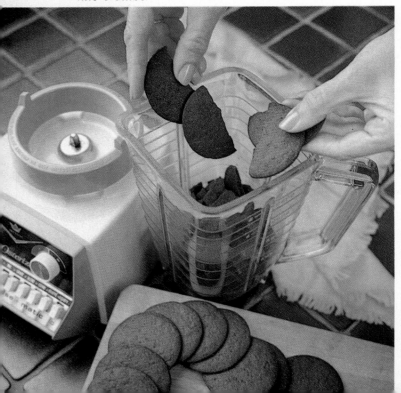

Chocolate Pudding & Pie Filling Mix

After you've used a wire whisk, you'll wonder how you ever got along without one.

1-1/2 cups plus 2 tablespoons unsweetened cocoa powder
3-1/4 cups granulated sugar

1-1/3 cups cornstarch
1/2 teaspoon salt

Press cocoa powder through a fine sieve. In a large bowl, combine all ingredients. Stir with a wire whisk until evenly distributed. Pour into a 6-cup container with a tight-fitting lid. Seal container. Label with date and contents. Store in a cool dry place. Use within 3 to 4 months. Makes about 6 cups CHOCOLATE PUDDING & PIE FILLING MIX.

CHOCOLATE PUDDING & PIE FILLING MIX makes:
Chocolate Cream Pie, page 120
Chocolate-Filled Pirouette Cookies, page 128
Creamy Chocolate Pudding, page 126
Layered Chocolate & Vanilla Dessert, page 122

Graham Cracker Crust Mix

With this mix, you'll crumb enough crackers for six crusts and have only one cleanup.

1 (2-lb.) box graham crackers
1 cup granulated sugar

2 teaspoons ground cinnamon

Process 6 or 7 crackers in blender to make fine crumbs. Pour crumbs into a large bowl. Repeat with remaining crackers. Or use a rolling pin to crush crackers between 2 sheets of waxed paper or in a plastic bag. Stir in sugar and cinnamon. Pour into a 10-cup container with a tight-fitting lid. Seal container. Label with date and contents. Store in a cool dry place. Use within 6 months. Makes about 9 cups GRAHAM CRACKER CRUST MIX.

GRAHAM CRACKER CRUST MIX makes:
Chocolate-Marshmallow Dessert, page 123
Chocolate-Peppermint Supreme, page 125
Graham Cracker Pie Crust, page 123
Lemon Light Dessert, page 124

Priscilla's Salad Dressing Mix

Make the dressing given below, then serve it over a spinach salad topped with crumbled bacon.

1/2 cup granulated sugar
1 teaspoon salt
1 teaspoon dry mustard

1 tablespoon poppy seeds
1 tablespoon dried minced onion

Combine all ingredients in a small bowl, stirring until evenly distributed. Pour into a 1/2-cup container with a tight-fitting lid or wrap airtight in heavy-duty foil. Seal container. Label with date and contents. Store in a cool dry place. Use within 3 months. Makes 1 package or about 1/3 cup PRISCILLA'S SALAD DRESSING MIX.

Priscilla's Salad Dressing

1-1/2 cups small-curd cottage cheese
(12 oz.)
1 pkg. PRISCILLA'S SALAD DRESSING
MIX, see above

1 cup vegetable oil
1/2 cup vinegar

Turn cottage cheese into a medium bowl; set aside. In a blender, combine PRISCILLA'S SALAD DRESSING MIX, oil and vinegar. Blend 5 to 8 seconds. Pour over cottage cheese. Fold oil mixture into cottage cheese until just blended. Cover; refrigerate 30 minutes before serving. Makes about 3 cups.

Spice Blend Mix

Add one teaspoon or more to cake batters, quick bread batters, whipped cream and pancakes.

2 tablespoons ground cinnamon
1 tablespoon ground nutmeg
1-1/2 teaspoons ground cloves
1-1/2 teaspoons ground allspice

1 tablespoon ground ginger
1 tablespoon dried grated orange or
lemon peel

In a 1/2-cup container with a tight-fitting lid, combine all ingredients. Attach lid. Label with date and contents. Store in a cool dry place. Use within 6 months. Makes about 6 tablespoons SPICE BLEND MIX.

French-Italian Salad Dressing Mix

Prepare several packages of mix at one time so they will be available when needed.

3 tablespoons granulated sugar
3/4 teaspoon salt
1/8 teaspoon ground pepper
1/2 teaspoon dry mustard

1/2 teaspoon paprika
1/2 teaspoon dried oregano leaves, crushed
1/8 teaspoon dried minced garlic
1-1/2 teaspoons dried minced onion

Cut a 6-inch square of heavy-duty foil. Place all ingredients in center of foil. Fold foil to make an airtight package. Label with date and contents. Store in a cool dry place. Use within 6 months. Makes 1 package or about 1/4 cup FRENCH-ITALIAN SALAD DRESSING MIX.

French-Italian Salad Dressing

l pkg. FRENCH-ITALIAN SALAD
** DRESSING MIX, see above**
1/2 cup vegetable oil

1/4 cup red wine vinegar
1/2 cup ketchup

In a blender, process FRENCH-ITALIAN SALAD DRESSING MIX, oil, vinegar and ketchup 5 to 7 seconds on high speed. Pour into a 2-cup container with a tight-fitting lid. Let stand at room temperature 5 hours. Refrigerate 30 minutes before serving. Makes about 1-1/4 cups.

FRENCH-ITALIAN SALAD DRESSING MIX makes: Apricot Chicken, page 93

How to Make Salad Dressing Mixes

1/Spoon measured ingredients onto foil for desired number of packages. Wrap and label.

2/Store seasoning mixes in small bottles, foil, plastic bags or containers with airtight lids.

Buttermilk & Onion Salad Dressing Mix

Dried minced onion is in smaller pieces than dried chopped onion.

1/2 cup dry buttermilk powder	**1 teaspoon monosodium glutamate, if desired**
1/4 teaspoon garlic powder	**1 teaspoon salt**
1 teaspoon onion powder	**1 tablespoon dried parsley leaves, crushed**
1 teaspoon dried minced onion	**1/4 teaspoon ground pepper**

Stir all ingredients in a small bowl until evenly distributed. Pour into a 1-cup container with a tight-fitting lid. Seal container. Label with date and contents. Store in a cool dry place. Use within 6 months. Makes 1 package or 2/3 cup BUTTERMILK & ONION SALAD DRESSING MIX.

Buttermilk & Onion Salad Dressing

1 pkg. BUTTERMILK & ONION	**2 cups mayonnaise**
SALAD DRESSING MIX, see above	**1 cup water**

In a large bowl, combine BUTTERMILK & ONION SALAD DRESSING MIX, mayonnaise and water, blending thoroughly. Pour into a 1-quart container with a tight-fitting lid. Refrigerate overnight. Makes about 3 cups.

Mary's Italian Dressing Mix

Fresh tomatoes or cucumbers are delicious when marinated in the dressing made from this mix.

1 teaspoon dried minced onion	**1/2 teaspoon celery seeds**
1 tablespoon dried parsley leaves, crushed	**1/4 teaspoon garlic powder**
1/4 teaspoon ground oregano	**2 tablespoons grated Parmesan cheese**
1/2 teaspoon dried sweet basil leaves, crushed	**1-1/2 teaspoons granulated sugar**
1/4 teaspoon ground thyme or ground marjoram	**1/8 teaspoon salt**
	Pinch ground pepper

Combine all ingredients in a small bowl, stirring until evenly distributed. Pour into a 1/4-cup container with a tight-fitting lid or wrap airtight in heavy-duty foil. Seal container. Label with date and contents. Store in a cool dry place. Use within 6 months. Makes 1 package or about 4 tablespoons MARY'S ITALIAN DRESSING MIX.

Mary's Italian Dressing

1 pkg. MARY'S ITALIAN DRESSING	**1/3 cup garlic wine vinegar**
MIX, see above	**3/4 cup vegetable oil**

In a small bowl or salad dressing cruet, combine MARY'S ITALIAN DRESSING MIX, vinegar and oil. Stir or shake until blended. Cover and refrigerate 30 minutes before serving. Makes about 1 cup.

Crisp Coating Mix

It takes about 8 cups corn flakes to make 3 cups corn flake crumbs.

3 cups corn flake crumbs
1 cup wheat germ
1/2 cup sesame seeds
4 teaspoons dried parsley leaves, crushed
1 tablespoon paprika

2 teaspoons salt
1 teaspoon dry mustard
1 teaspoon celery salt
1 teaspoon onion salt
1/2 teaspoon ground pepper

In a large bowl, combine all ingredients. Stir with a wire whisk until evenly distributed. Pour into a 5-cup container with a tight-fitting lid. Seal container. Label with date and contents. Store in a cool dry place. Use within 2 months. Makes about 4-1/2 cups CRISP COATING MIX.

CRISP COATING MIX makes:
Chicken & Ham Foldovers, page 95
Crunchy-Crust Chicken, page 94

Crunchy Fish Bake, page 91
Easy-Baked Pork Chops, page 97

Onion Seasoning Mix *Photo on page 12.*

Use this mix whenever your recipe calls for dry onion soup mix.

4 teaspoons instant beef bouillon granules
8 teaspoons dried minced onion

1 teaspoon onion powder
1/4 teaspoon bon appetit seasoning

Cut a 6-inch square of heavy-duty foil. Place all ingredients in center of foil. Fold foil to make an airtight package. Label with date and contents. Store in a cool dry place. Use within 6 months. Makes 1 package ONION SEASONING MIX.

ONION SEASONING MIX makes:
Apricot Chicken, page 93
Company Beef Brisket, page 96
Cowboy Beans, page 70
Football Hero, page 98

French Onion Soup Gratiné, page 61
Meat & Potato Pie, page 76
No-Fuss Swiss Steak Cubes, page 97
Onion Pot Roast, page 96

Crumble dried herb leaves in the palm of your hand to release the herb flavor.

Stuffing Seasoning Mix

Dried sage is available as dried leaves, ground sage and rubbed sage.

1 teaspoon ground sage or poultry seasoning
1 teaspoon instant chicken
   bouillon granules
1 tablespoon dried chopped celery

2 teaspoons dried minced onion
2 teaspoons dried parsley leaves, crushed
1/8 teaspoon ground pepper

Cut a 6-inch square of heavy-duty foil. Place all ingredients in center of foil. Fold foil to make an airtight package. Label with date and contents. Store in a cool dry place. Use within 6 months. Makes 1 package STUFFING SEASONING MIX.

Saucepan Stuffing

1-1/4 cups water
3 tablespoons butter or margarine
1 pkg. STUFFING SEASONING MIX,
   see above

4 cups partially dried 1/2-inch bread cubes

In a medium saucepan, combine water, butter or margarine and STUFFING SEASONING MIX. Bring to a boil over medium-high heat. Reduce heat to medium; simmer about 5 minutes. Stir in bread cubes. Cook 1 to 2 minutes until liquid is absorbed, stirring constantly. Cover; remove from heat. Let stand 5 minutes before serving. Makes 4 to 6 servings.

Variations

Whole-Wheat Stuffing: Substitute 2 cups partially dried whole-wheat bread pieces for half of bread cubes.
Cornbread Stuffing: Use 3 cups crumbled cornbread for bread cubes.
Granola Stuffing: Add 1/2 cup granola. Increase water to 1-1/2 cups.
Nut Stuffing: Add 1/4 cup walnuts or diced water chestnuts.

STUFFING SEASONING MIX makes: Stuffed Pork Chops, page 99

How to make a mixer bowl cover: With a bowl on the mixer, place a large paper plate on top of the bowl. Lower the mixer head. Mark on the paper plate where the posts of the beaters are to be inserted. Cut 1 or 2 holes in the plate slightly larger than needed for the beater posts to pass through and insert into the mixer. Insert the beater posts through the plate, then into the mixer. Hold the plate against the bowl while beating dry ingredients or other mixtures that splatter.

Small Family Pantry Mixes
Quick Mix

Whenever a recipe calls for biscuit mix, use this versatile mix.

4-1/4 cups all-purpose flour
2 tablespoons baking powder
1-1/2 teaspoons salt
1 teaspoon cream of tartar
1/2 teaspoon baking soda

3/4 cup instant nonfat milk powder or
 dry buttermilk powder
1 cup plus 2 tablespoons
 vegetable shortening

In a large bowl, combine flour, baking powder, salt, cream of tartar, baking soda and milk powder or buttermilk powder. Stir with a wire whisk to blend. Use a pastry blender, a heavy-duty mixer with a bowl cover or your fingers to blend in shortening until evenly distributed. Spoon into an 8-cup container with a tight-fitting lid. Seal container. Label with date and contents. Store in a cool dry place. Use within 10 to 12 weeks. Makes about 7 cups QUICK MIX.

QUICK MIX makes:
Quick Pancakes, page 138
Fruit Muffins, page 138

Light & Tender Biscuits, page 138

Chili Seasoning Mix

Include this mix in your camping supplies. It will season chili for two people.

1-1/2 teaspoons all-purpose flour
1 tablespoon dried minced onion
3/4 teaspoon chili powder
1/2 teaspoon seasoning salt

1/4 teaspoon crushed dried red pepper
1/4 teaspoon dried minced garlic
1/4 teaspoon granulated sugar
1/4 teaspoon ground cumin

Cut a 6-inch square of heavy-duty foil. Measure all ingredients onto foil. Fold foil to make an air-tight seal. Label with date and contents. Store in a cool dry place. Use within 6 months. Makes 1 package CHILI SEASONING MIX.

Quick Chili

1/2 lb. lean ground beef
1 (15-oz.) can kidney beans with liquid
1 (16-oz.) can tomatoes with liquid

1 pkg. CHILI SEASONING MIX,
 see above

Brown ground beef in a medium skillet over medium-high heat. Discard drippings. Stir in kidney beans, tomatoes and CHILI SEASONING MIX. Reduce heat; simmer 15 minutes, stirring occasionally. Makes 2 servings.

Spaghetti Seasoning Mix

One package makes spaghetti for two people. Make as many packages as you'll use in six months.

1-1/2 teaspoons dried minced onion
1-1/2 teaspoons dried parsley leaves,
  crushed
1-1/2 teaspoons cornstarch
1 teaspoon dried green pepper flakes

3/4 teaspoon salt
1/8 teaspoon dried minced garlic
1/2 teaspoon granulated sugar
1/4 teaspoon ground oregano
1/4 teaspoon ground basil

Cut a 6-inch square of heavy-duty foil; set aside. Combine all ingredients in a small bowl, stirring until evenly distributed. Pour mixture onto foil. Fold foil to make an airtight package. Label with date and contents. Store in a cool dry place. Use within 6 months. Makes 1 package SPAGHETTI SEASONING MIX.

Quick Spaghetti Sauce

1/2 lb. lean ground beef
1 (8-oz.) can tomato sauce
3 tablespoons tomato paste

1-1/3 cups tomato juice or water
1 pkg. SPAGHETTI SEASONING MIX,
  see above

Brown ground beef in a medium skillet over medium-high heat. Drain. Add tomato sauce, tomato paste and tomato juice or water. Stir in SPAGHETTI SEASONING MIX. Reduce heat; simmer 30 minutes, stirring occasionally. Makes 2 servings.

Chicken Continental Rice Mix

One package of mix makes a side dish to serve two people.

1/2 cup uncooked long-grain rice
1-1/2 teaspoons dried minced onion
1/4 teaspoon salt
1 teaspoon dried parsley leaves, crushed
1/8 teaspoon ground thyme

1 teaspoon instant chicken
  bouillon granules
1 teaspoon dried celery flakes
Pinch ground pepper

Combine all ingredients in a 1/2-cup container with a tight-fitting lid. Seal container. Label with date and contents. Store in a cool dry place. Use within 6 months. Makes 1 package CHICKEN CONTINENTAL RICE MIX, about 1/2 cup.

Chicken Continental Rice

1 cup water
1 teaspoon butter or margarine

1 pkg. CHICKEN CONTINENTAL
  RICE MIX, see above

Combine water and butter or margarine in a small saucepan. Bring to a boil. Stir in CHICKEN CONTINENTAL RICE MIX. Cover tightly. Reduce heat to low. Cook 20 to 25 minutes until liquid is absorbed and rice is tender. Makes 2 servings.

Corn Bread Mix *Photo on page 12.*

Cornbread baked in glass, cast-iron or a dark metal pan develops a golden-brown crust.

2 cups all-purpose flour
2 cups yellow cornmeal
1 cup instant nonfat milk powder or
   dry buttermilk powder

1/3 cup granulated sugar
2 tablespoons baking powder
1-1/2 teaspoons salt
1-1/2 teaspoons baking soda

In a large bowl, combine all ingredients, stirring with a wire whisk until evenly distributed. Pour into a 5-cup container with a tight-fitting lid. Seal container. Label with date and contents. Store in a cool dry place. Use within 10 to 12 weeks. Makes about 5 cups CORN BREAD MIX.

CORN BREAD MIX makes:
Corn Bread, page 134
Quick Corn Dogs, page 132

Hot Cocoa Mix *Photo on page 12.*

Stir 3 to 4 tablespoons mix into one cup hot water to make one serving.

1 cup powdered sugar
1/2 cup unsweetened cocoa powder
1/2 cup non-dairy cream powder

1/4 teaspoon salt
2-3/4 cups instant nonfat milk powder
1 cup miniature marshmallows, if desired

In a sifter, combine powdered sugar, cocoa powder, non-dairy cream powder and salt. Sift into a large bowl. Stir in milk powder and marshmallows, if desired. Pour into a 4-cup container with a tight-fitting lid. Seal container. Label with date and contents. Store in a cool dry place. Use within 6 months. Makes about 4 cups HOT COCOA MIX.

Crumb Cake Mix *Photo on page 12.*

When you're cooking for more than one or two, double the cake recipes listed below.

3-1/2 cups all-purpose flour
2-1/2 cups granulated sugar
2 tablespoons cornstarch

3-1/2 tablespoons baking powder
3/4 teaspoon salt
1-1/2 cups vegetable shortening

In a large sifter, combine flour, sugar, cornstarch, baking powder and salt. Sift into a large bowl. Use a pastry blender, a heavy-duty mixer with a bowl cover or your fingers to blend in shortening until evenly distributed. Spoon into an 8-cup container with a tight-fitting lid. Seal container. Label with date and contents. Store in a cool dry place. Use within 10 to 12 weeks. Makes about 8 cups CRUMB CAKE MIX.

CRUMB CAKE MIX makes:
Chocolate Crumb Cake, page 136
Lemon Pound Cake, page 135

Yellow Crumb Cake, page 136

High Health Pantry Mixes

Granola Mix   Photo on cover.

You will find triticale, rye and wheat flakes in many supermarkets and health foods stores.

3-1/2 cups old-fashioned or
   quick-cooking rolled oats
1/2 cup triticale flakes
1/2 cup rye flakes
1/2 cup wheat flakes
3/4 cup wheat germ
1 cup shredded coconut
3/4 cup shelled raw or
   toasted sunflower seeds
1-1/2 cups finely chopped mixed nuts
1/2 cup sesame seeds, if desired

1/4 to 1/2 cup packed dark brown sugar
3/4 cup water
3/4 cup vegetable oil
1/4 cup honey
1/4 cup molasses
3/4 teaspoon salt
1 teaspoon ground cinnamon
1-1/2 teaspoons vanilla extract
2 cups raisins, chopped dates or
   other dried fruit, if desired

Preheat oven to 300°F (150°C). In a large bowl, combine oats, triticale flakes, rye flakes, wheat flakes, wheat germ, coconut, sunflower seeds, nuts and sesame seeds, if desired. Stir until evenly distributed. In a medium saucepan, combine brown sugar, water, oil, honey, molasses, salt, cinnamon and vanilla. Heat and stir until sugar is dissolved. Do not boil. Pour syrup over oats mixture. Stir with a large wooden spoon until syrup coats other ingredients. Spread mixture in two 13" x 9" baking pans or on 2 large baking sheets with raised sides. Bake 20 to 30 minutes in preheated oven, stirring occasionally. Bake 10 minutes longer for a crunchier texture. Cool on racks. Stir in raisins, chopped dates or other dried fruit, if desired. Spoon into a 10-cup container with a tight-fitting lid. Seal container. Label with date and contents. Store in a cool dry place. Use within 6 months. Makes about 10 cups GRANOLA MIX.

Variation
Increase rolled oats to 5 cups. Omit triticale flakes, rye flakes and wheat flakes.

GRANOLA MIX makes:
Chicken with Fruit Stuffing, page 145
Good-For-You-Gems, page 147
Granola Energy Bars, page 148

Granola Fruit Crisp, page 148
TRAIL MIX, page 26

Homemade nutri-nuts are more moist than the commercial product similar to them.

Nutri-Nut Cereal Mix   *Photo on page 12.*

The nutri-nuts will still be slightly moist after the final baking.

2 cups whole-wheat flour
2 cups yellow cornmeal
2 cups quick-cooking rolled oats
2 cups unbleached or all-purpose flour
2 teaspoons baking powder

2 teaspoons salt
1/2 cup packed dark brown sugar
1 cup dark unsulphured molasses or sorghum
2-1/2 cups fresh milk

Preheat oven to 300°F (150°C). Lightly grease two 13" x 9" baking pans; set aside. In a large bowl, combine whole-wheat flour, cornmeal and oats, stirring with a wire whisk. In a sifter, combine unbleached or all-purpose flour, baking powder and salt. Sift into whole-wheat flour mixture. Stir in brown sugar. In a small bowl, combine molasses or sorghum and milk. Stir to blend. Stir into other ingredients until evenly distributed. Spread about 1/2 inch thick in prepared baking pans. Bake 1 hour in preheated oven. Remove from oven. Turn off oven. Cut in 2-inch squares with pizza cutter or a sharp knife. Cool about 2 hours. Preheat oven to 275°F (135°C). Using a coarse blade, put nutri-nut squares through a food grinder or process in a blender to make coarse crumbs. Return to pans. Toast in oven about 30 minutes until nearly dry. Store in a 14-cup container with a tight-fitting lid. Seal container. Label with date and contents. Use within 10 to 12 weeks. Makes about 13 cups NUTRI-NUT CEREAL MIX.

NUTRI-NUT CEREAL MIX makes:
Breakfast Parfait, page 142
Good-for-You-Gems, page 147
Irresistible Apple, page 146

Nutri-Nut Breakfast Bars, page 139
TRAIL MIX, page 26

Spiced Oatmeal Mix   *Photo on page 12.*

Dried fruits should still be soft, moist and pliable with no pockets of moisture.

8 cups quick-cooking rolled oats
1/2 cup packed brown sugar
2 teaspoons salt

2-1/2 teaspoons ground cinnamon
1-1/2 teaspoons ground nutmeg
1-1/2 cups dried apple pieces or raisins

Combine all ingredients in a large bowl, stirring with a wire whisk until evenly distributed. Pour into a 10-cup container with a tight-fitting lid. Seal container. Label with date and contents. Store in a cool dry place. Use within 6 months. Makes about 10 cups SPICED OATMEAL MIX.

SPICED OATMEAL MIX makes:
Spiced Oatmeal, page 142
Spicy Oatmeal Pancakes, page 140

Swiss Porridge, page 140

Trail Mix

Take some of this nutritious mix with you when you go hiking or camping.

1/2 cup dried apples, dried prunes or
   dried apricots or combination
2 cups GRANOLA MIX, page 24 or
   NUTRI-NUT CEREAL MIX, page 25

1 cup mixed nuts
1/2 cup chopped dates or raisins

Cut four 12" x 10" pieces of heavy-duty foil; set aside. Or set aside 4 medium-size, heavy plastic bags. Cut dried fruit into bite-size pieces. In a large bowl, combine all ingredients. Divide into 1 cup portions. Pour onto foil pieces or into plastic bags. Seal to make airtight packages. Label with date and contents. Store in a cool dry place. Makes about 4 cups TRAIL MIX.

Garden Herb Dressing Mix

Spike, an herbal seasoning salt, can be purchased in health food stores.

2 teaspoons dried parsley leaves
2 teaspoons dried basil leaves
Pinch ground cumin
1 teaspoon spike

1/8 teaspoon garlic powder
Pinch ground oregano
Pinch ground pepper
1/4 teaspoon dried minced onion

Cut a 6-inch square of heavy-duty foil. Combine ingredients on foil. Fold foil to make an airtight package. Label with date and contents. Store in a cool dry place. Use within 6 months. Makes 1 package or about 2 tablespoons GARDEN HERB DRESSING MIX.

Garden Herb Dressing

1 pkg. GARDEN HERB DRESSING MIX,
   see above
1/4 cup cider vinegar

2 tablespoons water
3/4 cup vegetable oil

Combine ingredients in a 2-cup container with a tight-fitting lid. Shake until blended. Refrigerate 30 minutes before serving. Makes about 1-1/4 cups.

One tablespoon fresh minced herbs equals 1 teaspoon dried herbs.

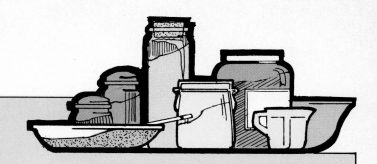

Refrigerator Mixes

Refrigerator mixes are more fragile than pantry mixes because of moisture content. As they are used, return mixes to the refrigerator as soon as possible. Because these mixes spoil rapidly if stored above 40°F (5°C), never let them sit on the counter or become warm. Storage times in the recipes are based on these temperatures.

Store refrigerator mixes according to space available in your refrigerator. If space is limited, cut larger recipes such as OATMEAL MUFFIN MIX and WHEAT & BRAN MUFFIN MIX in half. Use plastic or glass containers with tight-fitting lids to keep refrigerator odors from penetrating the mixes. As you plan menus, include recipes made from refrigerator mixes so the mixes will be used within the suggested time. Menu-planning suggestions are in *Sample Menus for One Month,* pages 6 and 7.

Shelf-life of some refrigerator mixes is increased to about six months by freezing. Package your mixes for freezing in amounts called for in specific recipes. Do not freeze OATMEAL MUFFIN MIX, WHEAT & BRAN MUFFIN MIX, CHEF'S SALAD DRESSING MIX and COOL CARROTS MIX. Their contents will not tolerate freezing.

Making quick, smooth and delicious gravies takes only minutes with BEEF GRAVY MIX and CHICKEN GRAVY MIX. When you want a rich, savory sauce for casseroles or to moisten meat or a vegetable, make the gravy as directed or sprinkle about 1/2 cup mix over the food and stir in 3/4 to 1 cup cold water. If there is water already on the food, retain about 1 cup, draining off the excess or use more mix.

ORIENTAL STIR-FRY MIX, one of our favorite refrigerator mixes, contains cornstarch. When cornstarch is mixed with liquid, a temporary suspension is formed. As it sits, starch settles, making a heavy layer. Stir the mixture thoroughly before removing amounts called for in recipes. As the mixture heats, stir continually to prevent lumps from forming.

Basic Refrigerator Mixes

Chocolate Syrup Mix

Add 2 tablespoons CHOCOLATE SYRUP MIX to a glass of cold milk for a refreshing chocolate drink.

1-1/3 cups unsweetened cocoa powder
2-1/4 cups granulated sugar
1/4 teaspoon salt

1-1/3 cups boiling water
1-1/2 teaspoons vanilla extract

In a heavy saucepan, combine cocoa powder, sugar and salt. Gradually stir in boiling water. Stir frequently over medium heat until smooth and slightly thickened, about 10 minutes. Remove from heat. Stir in vanilla. Pour mixture into a 3-cup container with a tight-fitting lid. Attach lid. Label container with date and contents. Store in refrigerator. Use within 10 to 12 weeks. Makes about 2-2/3 cups CHOCOLATE SYRUP MIX.

CHOCOLATE SYRUP MIX makes:
Chocolate Chip Ice Cream, page 126
Quick Fudge Sauce, page 123

Chocolate Ice Cream Soda, page 126

Chicken Gravy Mix

Instant bouillon granules and instant flour are available in most supermarkets.

1-1/3 cups instant nonfat milk powder
3/4 cup instant flour
3 tablespoons instant chicken
    bouillon granules

1/4 teaspoon ground sage
1/8 teaspoon ground thyme
1/8 teaspoon ground pepper
1/2 cup butter or margarine

In a medium bowl, combine milk powder, flour, bouillon granules, sage, thyme and pepper. Stir with a wire whisk until blended. Use a pastry blender or 2 knives to cut in butter or margarine until evenly distributed. Spoon into a 3-cup container with a tight-fitting lid. Attach lid. Label with date and contents. Store in refrigerator. Use within 4 to 6 weeks. Makes about 2-2/3 cups CHICKEN GRAVY MIX.

Chicken Gravy

1 cup cold water
1/2 cup CHICKEN GRAVY MIX, see above

Pour water into a small saucepan. Use a wire whisk to stir CHICKEN GRAVY MIX into water. Stir constantly over medium heat until gravy is smooth and slightly thickened, 2 to 3 minutes. Makes about 1 cup.

CHICKEN GRAVY MIX makes:
Chicken Breasts en Croûte, page 94
Chicken in Mushroom Sauce, page 94

Turkey Dinner Pie, page 76
Chicken & Ham Foldovers, page 95

Chef's Salad Dressing Mix

Granulated garlic is dried garlic ground as fine as salt crystals.

2-1/2 cups mayonnaise
1-1/2 cups fresh buttermilk
2 tablespoons vinegar
2 tablespoons granulated sugar
1/2 teaspoon Worcestershire sauce

1/4 teaspoon dry mustard
1/2 teaspoon salt
1/8 teaspoon granulated garlic or
    garlic powder

In a medium bowl, combine all ingredients. Stir with a wire whisk until thoroughly blended. Pour into a 1-quart container with a tight-fitting lid. Attach lid. Label with date and contents. Store in refrigerator. Use within 4 weeks. Makes about 1 quart CHEF'S SALAD DRESSING MIX.

CHEF'S SALAD DRESSING MIX makes:
Thousand Island Dressing, page 65
Blue Cheese Dressing, page 65

Sweet Lime Dressing, page 65

Sour Cream & Cheese Mix   *Photo on page 30.*

Try this mix as a topping on your favorite cooked vegetables.

3 cups shredded Cheddar cheese (12 oz.)
1-1/2 cups dairy sour cream
3/4 cup butter or margarine, softened

2 tablespoons chopped green onion tops
  or chopped chives
3/4 teaspoon salt

In a large bowl, combine all ingredients. Stir with a wire whisk to blend. Spoon into a 5-cup container with a tight-fitting lid. Attach lid. Label container with date and contents. Store in refrigerator. Use within 2 weeks. Makes about 5 cups SOUR CREAM & CHEESE MIX.

SOUR CREAM & CHEESE MIX makes:
Glorified Baked Potatoes, page 68
Tangy Cauliflower, page 68

Cool Carrots Mix   *Photos on page 30 and cover.*

Add this colorful mixture to a tossed vegetable salad or serve it as a condiment.

2 lb. carrots, sliced, cooked, drained
  (about 4 cups cooked)
2 small green peppers, cut in slivers
2 small onions, sliced, separated in rings
1 (10-1/2-oz.) can tomato soup or
  1 (8-oz.) can tomato sauce
1/2 cup vinegar

1/2 cup vegetable oil
1 cup granulated sugar
1/2 teaspoon dry mustard
1/2 teaspoon salt
1 teaspoon Worcestershire sauce
Pinch ground pepper

In a 2-quart glass container with a tight-fitting lid, layer cooked carrots, green pepper slivers and onion rings; set aside. In a small saucepan, combine tomato soup or tomato sauce, vinegar, oil, sugar, dry mustard, salt, Worcestershire sauce and pepper. Bring to a boil over medium heat, stirring occasionally. Pour tomato mixture over layered vegetables. Attach lid. Label container with date and contents. Store in refrigerator. Use within 2 weeks. Makes about 6 cups COOL CARROTS MIX.

Marinated Carrot Salad

2 large lettuce leaves
1-1/2 cups COOL CARROTS MIX,
  see above

2 hard-cooked eggs, sliced
1 tomato, cut in wedges
2 ripe olives for garnish

Arrange lettuce leaves on 2 salad plates. Spoon COOL CARROTS MIX evenly on lettuce leaves. Garnish salads evenly with egg slices, tomato wedges and olives. Makes 2 servings.

Marinade Blend Mix

This mix also makes an excellent salad dressing.

1 cup cider vinegar
1 cup vegetable oil
1/2 cup granulated sugar
4-1/2 teaspoons onion salt
1 tablespoon garlic salt
1-1/2 teaspoons ground thyme
1 teaspoon dried rosemary leaves

1 teaspoon dried sweet basil leaves
1 teaspoon capers with liquid
1/2 teaspoon dill seeds
1/4 cup frozen orange juice concentrate, thawed
4 tablespoons lemon juice

Combine all ingredients in blender. Process 1 minute on high speed. Pour into a 1-quart container with a tight-fitting lid. Attach lid. Label container with date and contents. Store in refrigerator. Use within 6 to 8 weeks. Makes about 3 cups MARINADE BLEND MIX.

MARINADE BLEND MIX makes:
Marinated Mushrooms, page 68
Marinated Flank Steak, page 97

Marinated Bean Salad, page 67

Beef Gravy Mix

There are at least two brown gravy flavoring sauces available in your supermarket.

1-1/3 cups instant nonfat milk powder
3/4 cup instant flour
3 tablespoons instant beef
    bouillon granules
1/8 teaspoon ground thyme

1/4 teaspoon onion powder
1/8 teaspoon ground sage
1/2 cup butter or margarine
3 teaspoons brown sauce for gravy

In a medium bowl, combine milk powder, flour, bouillon granules, thyme, onion powder and sage. Stir with a wire whisk to blend. Use a pastry blender or 2 knives to cut in butter or margarine until evenly distributed. Drizzle brown sauce for gravy over mixture. Stir with wire whisk until blended. Spoon into a 3-cup container with a tight-fitting lid. Attach lid. Label container with date and contents. Store in refrigerator. Use within 4 to 6 weeks. Makes about 2-2/3 cups BEEF GRAVY MIX.

Beef Gravy

1 cup cold water
1/2 cup BEEF GRAVY MIX, see above

Pour water into a small saucepan. Use a wire whisk to stir BEEF GRAVY MIX into water. Stir constantly over medium heat until gravy is smooth and slightly thickened, 2 to 3 minutes. Makes about 1 cup.

BEEF GRAVY MIX makes:
Tasty Beef Roll-Ups, page 98
Smothered Hamburger Patties, page 90

Stuffed Porkchops, page 99

Marinated Bean Salad, page 67, with SOUR CREAM & CHEESE MIX, page 29, COOL CARROTS MIX, page 29, and MARINADE BLEND MIX, above.

Oriental Stir-Fry Mix

Cut the bark-like skin off the ginger root, then shred the root on a fine-hole grater.

6 tablespoons cornstarch
3/4 teaspoon garlic powder
**2-1/4 teaspoons instant beef
    bouillon granules**
3/4 teaspoon onion powder
6 tablespoons wine vinegar

6 tablespoons water
1-1/2 teaspoons freshly grated ginger
3/4 cup soy sauce
3/4 cup dark corn syrup
2-2/3 cups water

In a large bowl, combine cornstarch, garlic powder, bouillon granules and onion powder. Use a wire whisk to stir in vinegar, 6 tablespoons water and ginger until cornstarch is dissolved. Stir in soy sauce, corn syrup and 2-2/3 cups water. Pour into a 5-cup container with a tight-fitting lid. Attach lid. Label container with date and contents. Store in refrigerator. Use within 4 weeks. *Stir well before using.* Makes about 5 cups ORIENTAL STIR-FRY MIX.

ORIENTAL STIR-FRY MIX makes:
Teriyaki Beef & Vegetables, page 84   Stir-Fry Cashew Chicken, page 80
Shrimp & Vegetable Stir-Fry, page 90

How to Grate Fresh Ginger

1/Cut or lightly scrape bark-like skin from ginger with paring knife or peeler.

2/Use small side of grater to finely grate ginger. Wrap and freeze remaining ginger to use later.

High Health Refrigerator Mixes
Whole-Wheat Hot Roll Mix   *Photo on cover.*

All-purpose flour can be substituted for the whole-wheat and unbleached flours.

9 cups whole-wheat flour
8 cups unbleached flour or
  all-purpose flour
4 teaspoons salt

1 cup instant nonfat milk powder
1 cup packed brown sugar or
  1 cup granulated sugar

In a large bowl, combine whole-wheat flour, unbleached or all-purpose flour, salt and milk powder. Stir with a wire whisk until evenly distributed. Press brown sugar through a coarse sieve. Stir brown sugar or granulated sugar into flour mixture. Pour into an 18-cup container with a tight-fitting lid. Attach lid. Label container with date and contents. Store in refrigerator 10 to 12 weeks or in freezer up to 6 months. Makes about 18 cups WHOLE-WHEAT HOT ROLL MIX.

WHOLE-WHEAT HOT ROLL MIX makes:

Bagels, page 106
Bread Basket Stew, page 79
Football Hero Bun, page 104
French Bread, page 103
Giant Braided Loaf, page 104
Hamburger Buns, page 100

Whole-Wheat Parker House Rolls, page 107
Pocket Bread, page 101
Swedish Rye Bread, page 107
Thin Wheat Crackers, page 55
Whole-Wheat Cinnamon Rolls, page 102

Honey & Wheat Mix

Honey and wheat—what a delicious combination.

3 cups whole-wheat flour
6 cups unbleached flour or
  all-purpose flour
1 cup instant nonfat milk powder or
  dry buttermilk powder

1/3 cup baking powder
4 teaspoons salt
2 cups vegetable shortening
1/4 cup honey

In a large bowl, combine whole-wheat flour, unbleached or all-purpose flour, milk powder or buttermilk powder, baking powder and salt. Use a pastry blender, a heavy-duty mixer with a bowl cover or your fingers to blend in shortening until evenly distributed. Texture will resemble corn-meal. Drizzle honey over mixture while beating with mixer on low speed or while stirring with a wire whisk. Spoon into a 12-cup container with a tight-fitting lid. Attach lid. Label container with date and contents. Use within 10 to 12 weeks if stored in refrigerator or within 6 months, if stored in freezer. Makes about 12 cups HONEY & WHEAT MIX.

HONEY & WHEAT MIX makes:
Honey & Wheat Muffins, page 143
Delicious Wheat Pancakes, page 140

Waffles with Pioneer Syrup, page 142
Buttermilk Biscuits, page 143

Oatmeal Muffin Mix

Muffins are easy to prepare with this flavorful mix.

2-1/2 cups whole-wheat flour
1-1/4 cups unbleached or all-purpose flour
4 teaspoons baking soda
3/4 teaspoon salt
4 cups quick-cooking rolled oats

2-1/4 cups boiling water
3/4 cup vegetable oil
1-1/4 cups packed brown sugar
3 eggs, slightly beaten
3 cups fresh buttermilk

In a medium bowl, combine whole-wheat flour, unbleached flour or all-purpose flour, baking soda and salt. Stir with a wire whisk to blend; set aside. Measure oats into a large bowl. Pour boiling water over oats. Let cool about 10 minutes. Add oil, brown sugar, eggs and buttermilk. Beat vigorously by hand or with an electric mixer about 1 minute to blend. Stir in flour mixture by hand until just blended. Pour into a 12-cup container with a tight-fitting lid. Attach lid. Label container with date and contents. Store in refrigerator. Use within 6 weeks. Makes about 12 cups OATMEAL MUFFIN MIX or about 50 muffins.

Baking instructions: Preheat oven to 375°F (190°C). Generously grease 12 muffin cups. Gently stir OATMEAL MUFFIN MIX. Fill prepared muffin cups about 3/4 full. Bake about 25 minutes in preheated oven until golden brown. Makes 12 muffins.

Variation

For each 1 cup of OATMEAL MUFFIN MIX used, stir in 1/4 cup chopped nuts, shredded coconut or dried fruit.

Wheat & Bran Muffin Mix

Reconstituted buttermilk powder is an economical substitute for fresh buttermilk used in baking.

1 cup vegetable oil
1 cup granulated sugar
4 eggs, beaten
2 cups water
4 cups whole-bran cold cereal
5 teaspoons baking soda

1 qt. fresh buttermilk
2 cups 40% bran flakes cereal
1 tablespoon salt
3 cups unbleached flour or
  all-purpose flour
2 cups whole-wheat flour

In a large bowl, combine oil and sugar. Beat in eggs; set aside. In a medium saucepan, bring water to a boil. Remove from heat. Stir in whole-bran cereal. Let soften 5 minutes. Stir baking soda and buttermilk into whole-bran cereal mixture. Immediately stir into sugar mixture. Stir in bran flakes, salt, unbleached or all-purpose flour and whole-wheat flour. Pour into a 12-cup container with a tight-fitting lid. Attach lid. Label container with date and contents. Store in refrigerator. Use within 6 weeks. Makes about 12 cups WHEAT & BRAN MUFFIN MIX or about 50 muffins.

Baking instructions: Preheat oven to 400°F (205°C). Generously grease 12 muffin cups. Stir muffin mix. Fill prepared muffin cups 3/4 full. Bake 15 to 20 minutes in preheated oven until browned. Makes 12 muffins.

Molasses & Bran Muffin Mix

Save time by beating the bran cereal and flour mixture with a heavy-duty mixer.

1 cup dry buttermilk powder
1-1/2 cups whole-wheat flour
1-1/2 cups unbleached flour or
   all-purpose flour
2 tablespoons baking soda

1 tablespoon salt
1-1/4 cups packed brown sugar
6 cups whole-bran cold cereal
6 tablespoons molasses

In a large bowl, combine buttermilk powder, whole-wheat flour, unbleached or all-purpose flour, baking soda and salt. Stir with a wire whisk to blend. Press brown sugar through a coarse sieve. Use a wire whisk to stir brown sugar into flour mixture until evenly distributed. Process whole-bran cereal in blender 1 cup at a time until coarse crumbs form. Stir cereal crumbs into flour mixture. Slowly pour molasses over mixture while stirring with a wire whisk or with a heavy-duty mixer on low speed, until evenly distributed. Spoon into a 10-cup container with a tight-fitting lid. Attach lid. Label container with date and contents. Use within 12 weeks if stored at room temperature or within 6 months if stored in refrigerator or freezer. Makes about 10 cups MOLASSES & BRAN MUFFIN MIX.

MOLASSES & BRAN MUFFIN MIX makes: Bran-ana Muffins, page 143

How to Make Molasses & Bran Muffin Mix

1/Process bran in blender or beat it and other dry ingredients with a heavy-duty mixer.

2/Stirring continually, drizzle molasses 1 tablespoon at a time into mixture.

Freezer Mixes

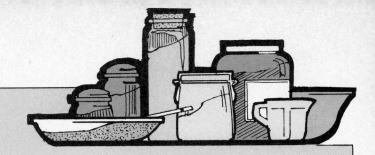

Cool cooked mixes 15 to 30 minutes, then refrigerate them one hour before freezing. They must be cooled quickly to retard growth of bacteria and preserve flavor. Foods become dry and tasteless if not properly packaged in moisture-vapor-proof containers.

Store frozen foods at 0°F (−18°C) or lower. For each five degrees above this temperature, food storage time is cut in half. Some refrigerator compartments will freeze ice and keep ready-frozen foods for about two weeks, but cannot freeze foods solid from the unfrozen state.

Freeze only one cooked mix at a time. For instance, CHILI BEANS & WHEAT MIX makes eight 2-cup packages. These eight packages should be completely frozen before adding more packages. Arrange new packages throughout the freezer where air can circulate around them until frozen. Put recipe page numbers on mix labels for ease in locating the recipe.

Rotate mixes so none get lost in the freezer. See *Sample Inventory*, page 5.

Thaw foods in the refrigerator, on the counter, on top of the stove or in a microwave oven. Counter thawing must be completed within four hours to prevent dangerous growth of bacteria. Use mixes as soon as they are thawed. *Never refreeze mixes.*

Basic Freezer Mixes

Freezer Cheese Sauce Mix

Try topping baked potatoes with this mix, then sprinkle with crumbled cooked bacon.

3/4 cup all-purpose flour
1-1/2 teaspoons salt
1/4 teaspoon ground nutmeg
3/4 cup butter or margarine
4 cups milk

2 cups condensed chicken broth
1 cup half-and-half
4 egg yolks, beaten
3 cups shredded Cheddar cheese (12 oz.)

In a small bowl, combine flour, salt and nutmeg; set aside. In a heavy large saucepan, melt butter or margarine over medium heat. Gradually stir in flour mixture, milk and chicken broth until smooth. Cook and stir over medium-high heat until smooth and slightly thickened, about 2 minutes. Remove from heat. In a medium bowl, stir half-and-half into egg yolks. Blend in about half of the hot sauce. Stir egg mixture into remaining sauce. Cook and stir over medium heat about 2 minutes; do not boil. Remove from heat. Stir in cheese until melted. Cool to room temperature. Refrigerate sauce until completely cooled. Pour about 1-1/3 cups sauce into each of 6 freezer containers with tight-fitting lids. Leave 1-inch air space at top of each container. Attach lids. Label containers with date and contents. Store in freezer. Use within 6 months. Makes 6 packages or about 8 cups FREEZER CHEESE SAUCE MIX.

FREEZER CHEESE SAUCE MIX makes:
Cauliflower Fritters in Cheese Sauce,
   page 69
Cheese Fondue, page 54

English Poached Eggs & Ham, page 89
Old-Fashioned Vegetable Platter, page 70
Puffy Omelet, page 89

Cubed Beef Mix

Brown sauce for gravy adds flavor and color to meat dishes or meat gravies.

1/4 cup butter or margarine	**4 teaspoons instant**
5 lbs. boneless lean beef	**beef bouillon granules or**
3 medium onions, sliced	**4 beef bouillon cubes**
3/4 cup all-purpose flour	**1/2 teaspoon pepper**
About 3 cups water	**1 bay leaf**
2-1/2 teaspoons salt	**1 tablespoon brown sauce for gravy**

In a heavy large skillet, melt butter or margarine over medium high heat. Add beef cubes. Stirring occasionally, cook until lightly browned. Drain as drippings collect; reserve drippings. Add onions to browned beef cubes. Stirring occasionally, cook until onions are soft and golden, 10 to 15 minutes. Sprinkle flour over beef mixture. Stir gently until flour is absorbed, about 1 minute. Add water to drippings to make 4 cups liquid. Stir liquid mixture, salt, bouillon granules or bouillon cubes, pepper, bay leaf and brown sauce for gravy into beef mixture. Bring mixture to a boil, stirring occasionally to loosen drippings in pan. Cover; cook over low heat about 2 hours longer until beef is tender. Remove from heat. Cool on a rack. Ladle into four 2-cup freezer containers with tight-fitting lids, leaving 1/2-inch space at top of each. Attach lids. Label containers with date and contents. Store in freezer. Use within 6 months. Makes 4 packages or about 8 cups CUBED BEEF MIX.

CUBED BEEF MIX MAKES:

Beef Ragout, page 74
Quick Pepper Beef Cubes, page 77

Stroganoff Beef Crepes, page 88

All-Purpose Ground Beef Mix

This very basic mix can be used in most casseroles that call for a meat mixture.

5 lbs. lean ground beef	**2 cups chopped onions**
1 tablespoon salt	**1 cup diced green pepper**
2 cups chopped celery	

In a large pot or Dutch oven, brown ground beef over medium-high heat, stirring to break up meat. Drain; discard drippings. Stir in salt, celery, onions and green pepper. Cover; simmer over low heat until vegetables are crisp-tender, about 10 minutes. Remove from heat; cool on a rack. Ladle into six 2-cup freezer containers with tight-fitting lids, leaving 1/2-inch air space at top of each. Cut through mixture in each container with a knife several times to remove air pockets. Attach lids. Label containers with date and contents. Store in freezer. Use within 3 months. Makes 6 packages or about 12 cups ALL-PURPOSE GROUND BEEF MIX.

ALL-PURPOSE GROUND BEEF MIX makes:

Best-Ever Minestrone Soup, page 61
Bunwiches, page 88
Company Casserole, page 75
Dinner in-a-Pumpkin, page 73
Easy Beef Stroganoff, page 84
Hearty Beef Chowder, page 58

Hurry-up Curry, page 81
Mexican Delight, page 74
Oriental-Style Hamburger Skillet, page 86
Quick Chow Mein, page 87
Slumgullion, page 80

Italian-Style Meat Mix   *Photo on cover.*

Butchers often have pork bones they will give away.

3 lbs. sweet Italian sausage,
  cut in 2-inch lengths
2 (28-oz.) cans tomato puree
1 (28-oz.) can peeled tomatoes,
  slightly mashed
1-1/2 teaspoons dried sweet basil leaves,
  crushed
1-1/4 teaspoons dried parsley leaves,
  crushed

1 teaspoon granulated sugar
1/4 teaspoon ground pepper
1/2 teaspoon garlic powder
5 teaspoons grated Romano cheese
6 cups water
1-1/2 lbs. pork bones
Meatballs, see below

Meatballs:

1-1/2 lbs. lean ground beef
1/2 teaspoon dried sweet basil leaves,
  crushed
1/4 teaspoon onion powder
1/2 teaspoon dried parsley leaves, crushed

1/2 teaspoon salt
1/4 teaspoon ground pepper
1/2 cup soft breadcrumbs
1 egg, beaten

In a large skillet or Dutch oven, brown Italian sausage over medium-high heat, stirring occasionally. Simmer over low heat 20 to 25 minutes longer until meat is no longer pink. Drain, reserving 2 tablespoons drippings in skillet. Stir in tomato puree, tomatoes, basil, parsley, sugar, pepper, garlic powder, Romano cheese, water and pork bones. Cover; simmer 30 minutes over medium heat. Prepare meatballs. Spoon meatballs into tomato mixture. Bring to a boil over medium-high heat. Cover; simmer over low heat 5 to 6 hours until thickened. Remove pork bones. Cool meatball mixture in skillet on a rack. Spoon into freezer containers in amounts shown in recipes listed below. Leave 1/2 inch air space at top of each container. Attach lids. Label containers with date, contents and quantity. Store in freezer. Use within 6 months. Makes about 16 cups ITALIAN-STYLE MEAT MIX.

Meatballs:
Preheat oven to 400°F (205°C). Combine all ingredients in a medium bowl. Shape into 1-inch balls. Place meatballs on an ungreased baking sheet with raised sides. Bake 10 to 15 minutes in preheated oven until browned. Remove meatballs from baking sheet. Discard drippings.

ITALIAN-STYLE MEAT MIX makes:

Cubed Pork Mix

To get the most from your meat, have your butcher cube a center cut of pork shoulder.

1/4 cup butter or margarine
5 lbs. boneless lean pork, cubed
3 medium onions, sliced
3/4 cup all-purpose flour
About 3-1/2 cups water

4 teaspoons instant chicken
bouillon granules or
4 chicken bouillon cubes
2-1/2 teaspoons salt
1/2 teaspoon ground pepper

In a large skillet, melt butter or margarine over medium-high heat. Add pork cubes. Cook until lightly browned, stirring occasionally. Drain as drippings collect; reserve drippings. Add onions to browned pork cubes. Cook 10 to 15 minutes until onions are soft and golden, stirring occasionally. Sprinkle flour over pork mixture. Stir gently until flour is absorbed, about 1 minute. Add water to drippings to make 4 cups liquid. Stir liquid mixture, bouillon granules or bouillon cubes, salt and pepper into pork mixture. Bring mixture to a boil, stirring occasionally to loosen drippings in pan. Cover; cook over low heat about 2 hours longer until pork is tender. Remove from heat. Cool on a rack. Ladle mixture into five 2-cup freezer containers with tight-fitting lids, leaving 1/2-inch space at top of each. Attach lids. Label containers with date and contents. Store in freezer. Use within 6 months. Makes 5 packages or about 10 cups CUBED PORK MIX.

CUBED PORK MIX makes:
Hurry-Up Curry, page 81
Pork Chow Mein, page 86
Pork Noodles, page 72

Quick Chow Mein, page 87
Sweet and Sour Pork, page 86
Won Tons, page 56

How to Make Cubed Pork Mix

1/Add onions to browned meat. Cook until onions are tender. Simmer 2 hours with remaining ingredients.

2/Spoon into five 2-cup freezer containers, leaving a 1/2-inch space at top. Label and store in freezer.

White Sauce Butter-Balls

White sauce made from these butter-balls is smooth and delicious.

2 cups all-purpose flour
2 tablespoons salt

1/2 teaspoon ground white pepper
2 cups butter or margarine, softened

Line 2 baking sheets with waxed paper; set aside. In a sifter, combine flour, salt and white pepper. Sift into a large bowl. Use an electric mixer to cream in butter or margarine until smooth. Drop by heaping tablespoons onto prepared baking sheets. Place in freezer until butter-balls are frozen. Remove frozen balls from baking sheets. Place in a firm freezer container with a tight-fitting lid or in 1 or 2 heavy-duty plastic bags. Label container or plastic bags with date and contents. Return to freezer. Use within 6 months. Makes about 28 WHITE SAUCE BUTTER-BALLS.

WHITE SAUCE BUTTER-BALLS makes:
Basic White Sauce, page 63
Creamed Mushrooms in Toast Cups, page 72
Creamed Peas, page 67
Ring-Around-the-Tuna, page 81
Creamed Vegetables in-a-Ring, page 82

Creamed Celery Sauce, page 64
Creamed Chicken Sauce, page 64
Creamed Mushroom Sauce, page 62
Wrapped Chicken Breasts, page 93

How to Make White Sauce Butter-Balls

1/Use an electric mixer to beat butter or margarine into flour mixture until smooth.

2/Place frozen balls in plastic bags or freezer container with tight-fitting lid. Return to freezer.

Freezer Pie Crust Mix

If you usually use a 10-inch pie plate, divide the dough into 6 rolls instead of 7 rolls.

6 cups all-purpose flour
2 teaspoons salt
1 (1-lb.) can vegetable shortening
  (2-1/3 cups)

1 cup cold water

Cut seven 12-inch squares of plastic wrap or waxed paper and heavy-duty foil; set aside. In a large bowl, combine flour and salt. With pastry blender, cut in shortening until evenly distributed. Texture will resemble cornmeal. Add cold water all at once. Mix lightly with a fork until water is absorbed and mixture forms a ball. Divide dough into 7 equal portions. Shape each portion into a ball. Flatten each ball slightly. Wrap each flattened ball in 1 piece of plastic wrap or waxed paper. Place 1 wrapped ball on each piece of foil. Fold foil tightly against ball, making an airtight seal. Label each package with date and contents. Store in freezer. Use within 10 months. Makes 7 packages of FREEZER PIE CRUST MIX, enough for seven 8- or 9-inch single crust pies.

Freezer Pie Crust

To make single pie crust: Completely thaw 1 package FREEZER PIE CRUST MIX. If baking empty crust, preheat oven to 450°F (230°C). On a lightly floured surface or between two 12-inch pieces of lightly floured plastic wrap, roll out dough to an 11-inch circle. Dough will be quite thin. Remove plastic wrap if used. Carefully fit rolled-out dough into an 8- or 9-inch pie plate without stretching dough. Trim and flute edge. Prick crust with the tines of a fork. Bake about 10 minutes in preheated oven until lightly browned. Or add filling and bake according to filling directions. **To make double-crust pie**: Completely thaw 2 packages FREEZER PIE CRUST MIX. Prepare 1 ball of dough according to directions above; do not prick crust or flute edge. Turn filling into shell. Roll out top crust. Place over filling. Press edges together; flute pressed edges. Cut small slits in top crust to let steam escape. Bake according to directions for filling.

FREEZER PIE CRUST MIX makes:
Cherry-Almond Pie, page 118
Chocolate Cream Pie, page 120
Deep-Dish Pot Pie, page 77
Fresh Peach Pie, page 116
Meat & Potatoe Pie, page 76
Queen Pie, page 118

Sour Cream & Lemon Pie, page 117
Sour Cream & Raisin Pie, page 117
Spanish Cheese Pie, page 76
Turkey Dinner Pie, page 76
Vanilla Cream Pie, page 121

Five-Way Beef Mix   Photo on cover.

By using a food processor to dice or chop the vegetables, you'll cut the work in half.

5 lbs. lean ground beef or lean beef cubes
4 onions, chopped, or
   1 cup dried chopped onions
3 tablespoons vegetable oil if
   using beef cubes
About 1 cup water if using beef cubes
8 cups diced peeled potatoes
6 cups diced peeled carrots

1/3 cup cornstarch
1/2 cup cold water
1 (24-oz.) pkg. frozen peas,
   partially thawed
4 teaspoons seasoning salt
2 teaspoons ground sage
1 teaspoon salt
1 teaspoon ground pepper

Brown ground beef and onions in a large skillet over medium heat; set aside. Or heat oil in skillet; add beef cubes and onions. Cook until cubes are browned. Add about 1 cup water to browned beef cubes. Cover and simmer over low heat until tender, about 1 hour, adding more water if needed. Place potatoes and carrots in a 5-quart Dutch oven. Add water to barely cover. Bring to a boil. Simmer vegetables over medium heat until crisp-tender, about 15 minutes. Stir cornstarch into 1/2 cup cold water. Stir into vegetable mixture until liquid is slightly thickened. Stir in remaining ingredients. Stir in browned beef mixture. Cool on a rack. Ladle mix into four 6-cup freezer containers with tight-fitting lids, leaving 1/2-inch air space. Stir to remove air pockets. Attach lids. Label with date and contents. Store in freezer. Use within 2 months. Makes 4 packages or about 24 cups FIVE-WAY BEEF MIX.

FIVE-WAY BEEF MIX makes:

Bread Basket Stew, page 79
Deep-Dish Pot Pie, page 77
Grandma's Hamburger Soup, page 59

Swiss Hamburger Soup, page 63
Vegetable & Cheese Casserole, page 74

Slice & Bake Sugar Cookies

For a special treat, frost these cookies with Vanilla Buttercream Frosting, page 13.

2 cups butter or margarine, softened
2 cups granulated sugar
3 eggs
2 teaspoons vanilla extract

1 teaspoon lemon extract
6 cups all-purpose flour
1 teaspoon baking soda

Cut four 14" x 12" pieces of waxed paper or plastic wrap; set aside. In a large bowl, cream butter or margarine and sugar. Beat in eggs, vanilla and lemon extract until light and fluffy. In a large bowl, combine flour and baking soda. Gradually stir flour mixture into egg mixture until blended. Divide dough into 4 equal pieces. Shape each piece into an 8- to 10-inch roll. Wrap each roll in 1 piece of waxed paper or plastic wrap. Place wrapped rolls in a plastic freezer container with a tight-fitting lid, or wrap air-tight in a 14" x 12" piece of heavy-duty foil; label. Store in freezer. Use within 6 months. Makes 4 rolls of dough or about 12 dozen cookies.

To bake 1 roll of dough: Preheat oven to 350°F (175°C). Lightly grease 2 large baking sheets. Cut frozen dough into 1/4-inch slices. Place slices on prepared baking sheets about 1/2 inch apart. Sprinkle slices lightly with granulated sugar, if desired. Bake 8 to 10 minutes until edges start to brown. Remove cookies from baking sheets. Cool on wire racks. Makes about 36 cookies.

Slice & Bake Molasses-Ginger Cookies

For a different taste, brush the warm cookies with a lemon juice and powdered sugar glaze.

1 cup butter, margarine or shortening
1 cup packed brown sugar
2 teaspoons baking soda
2 teaspoons salt
2 teaspoons ground cinnamon
1 teaspoon ground ginger

1 teaspoon ground cloves
1 teaspoon ground allspice
6-1/2 cups all-purpose flour
2/3 cup water or apple cider
1-1/2 cups light-colored molasses

Cut four 14'' x 12'' pieces of waxed paper or plastic wrap; set aside. In large bowl, cream butter, margarine or shortening and sugar; set aside. In a large bowl, combine baking soda, salt, cinnamon, ginger, cloves, allspice and flour; set aside. Beat water or cider and molasses into sugar mixture. Gradually blend flour mixture into sugar mixture until distributed. Divide dough into 4 equal pieces. Shape each piece into an 8- to 10-inch roll. Wrap each roll in 1 piece of waxed paper or plastic wrap. Place wrapped rolls in a plastic freezer container with a tight-fitting lid, or wrap airtight in a 14'' x 12'' piece of heavy-duty foil. Label with date and contents. Store in freezer. Use within 6 months. Makes 4 rolls of dough or about 12 dozen cookies.

To bake 1 roll of dough: Preheat oven to 350°F (175°C). Lightly grease 2 large baking sheets. Cut frozen dough into 1/4-inch slices. Arrange slices on prepared baking sheets, about 1/2 inch apart. Bake about 8 minutes until slightly set on top. Remove cookies from baking sheets. Cool on wire racks. Makes about 36 cookies.

How to Shape and Wrap Freezer Cookies

1/Slightly dampen hands. Shape dough into four 8- to 10-inch rolls. Wrap in waxed paper or plastic wrap.

2/Place wrapped rolls in freezer container or wrap airtight in heavy duty foil. Label; freeze.

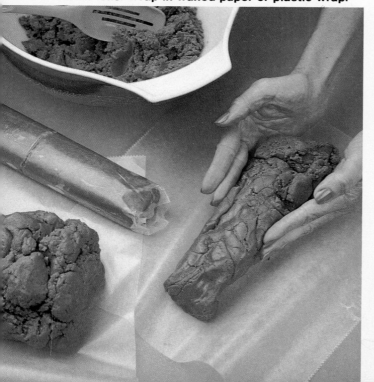

Slice & Bake Oatmeal Cookies

These oatmeal cookies will flatten slightly and be quite crisp.

1-1/2 cups vegetable shortening
1-1/2 cups granulated sugar
1-1/2 cups packed brown sugar
3 eggs
1-1/2 teaspoons vanilla extract
1-3/4 cups all-purpose flour

1-1/2 teaspoons salt
1-1/2 teaspoons baking soda
4-1/2 cups rolled oats, uncooked
3/4 cup chopped nuts
3/4 cup raisins

Cut four 14" x 12" pieces of waxed paper or plastic wrap. Cream shortening, granulated sugar and brown sugar in a large bowl until smooth. Beat in eggs and vanilla until light and fluffy. In a medium bowl, combine flour, salt and baking soda. Gradually stir flour mixture into egg mixture until blended. Stir in oats, nuts and raisins. Divide dough into 4 equal pieces. Shape each piece into an 8- to 10-inch roll. Wrap each roll in 1 piece of waxed paper or plastic wrap. Place wrapped rolls in a plastic freezer container with a tight-fitting lid, or wrap airtight in a 14" x 12" piece of heavy-duty foil. Label with date and contents. Store in freezer. Use within 6 months. Makes 4 rolls of dough or about 12 dozen cookies.

To bake 1 roll of dough: Preheat oven to 350°F (175°C). Lightly grease 2 large baking sheets; set aside. Cut frozen dough into 1/4-inch thick slices. Place slices about 1 inch apart on prepared baking sheets. Bake 10 to 12 minutes until edges are browned and centers are slightly set. Cool about 2 minutes on baking sheet. Remove cookies from baking sheets. Cool completely on wire racks. Makes about 36 cookies.

Slice & Bake Chocolate Wafer Cookies

Use these cookies to make ice cream sandwiches or Chocolate Wafer Pie Crust, page 120.

2 cups butter or margarine
2-1/2 cups granulated sugar
3 eggs
2 teaspoons vanilla extract

5 cups all-purpose flour
1 teaspoon baking soda
1-1/4 cups unsweetened cocoa powder

Cut four 14" x 12" pieces of waxed paper or plastic wrap; set aside. In a large bowl, beat butter or margarine, sugar, eggs and vanilla until light and fluffy. In a medium bowl, combine flour, baking soda and cocoa powder. Gradually stir flour mixture into sugar mixture until evenly distributed. Divide dough into 4 equal pieces. Shape each piece into an 8- to 10-inch roll. Wrap each roll in 1 piece of waxed paper or plastic wrap. Place wrapped rolls in a plastic freezer container with a tight-fitting lid, or wrap airtight in a 14" x 12" piece of heavy-duty foil. Label with date and contents. Store in freezer. Use within 6 months. Makes 4 rolls of dough or about 12 dozen cookies.

To bake 1 roll of dough: Preheat oven to 350°F (175°C). Lightly grease 2 large baking sheets. Slice frozen dough 1/4-inch thick. Arrange slices on prepared baking sheets about 1/2 inch apart. Bake 8 to 10 minutes until cookies are set on edges and slightly firm on top. Remove cookies from baking sheets. Cool on racks. Makes about 36 cookies.

Basket holds a medley of Slice & Bake Cookies, pages 42 to 46. SLICE & BAKE PEANUT BUTTER COOKIES, page 46, are on the board. SLICE & BAKE CHOCOLATE CHIP COOKIES, page 46, are in the container.

Slice & Bake Peanut Butter Cookies

Use a wire whisk to stir the flour and baking soda together.

2 cups vegetable shortening
2 cups granulated sugar
2 cups packed brown sugar
2 cups creamy or chunk-style peanut butter

2 teaspoons vanilla extract
4 eggs
5 cups all-purpose flour
4 teaspoons baking soda

Cut four 14" x 12" pieces of waxed paper or plastic wrap; set aside. Cream shortening, granulated sugar, brown sugar and peanut butter in a large bowl. Beat in vanilla and eggs until light and fluffy. In a large bowl, combine flour and baking soda. Gradually stir flour mixture into egg mixture until blended. Divide dough into 4 equal pieces. Shape each piece into an 8- to 10-inch roll. Wrap each roll in 1 piece of waxed paper or plastic wrap. Place wrapped rolls in a plastic freezer container with a tight-fitting lid, or wrap airtight in a 14" x 12" piece of heavy-duty foil. Label with date and contents. Store in freezer. Use within 6 months. Makes 4 rolls of dough or about 12 dozen cookies.

To bake 1 roll of dough: Let dough thaw slightly. Preheat oven to 350°F (175°C). Cut slightly thawed dough into 1-inch thick slices. Cut each slice into fourths. Roll each piece into a ball. Place balls on an ungreased baking sheet about 1-1/2 inches apart. Use tines of a fork to flatten cookies by pressing down in criss-cross fashion. Bake 8 to 10 minutes until lightly browned around edges. Remove from baking sheet. Cool on wire racks. Makes about 36 cookies.

Slice & Bake Chocolate Chip Cookies

It will be easier to shape the rolls of dough if you wet your hands.

2 cups butter or margarine
1-1/3 cups granulated sugar
1-2/3 cups packed brown sugar
1 tablespoon vanilla extract
4 eggs

5-1/2 cups all-purpose flour
2 teaspoons salt
2 teaspoons baking soda
2 cups semisweet chocolate pieces
1 cup chopped nuts

Cut four 14" x 12" pieces of waxed paper or plastic wrap; set aside. In a large bowl, cream butter or margarine, granulated sugar and brown sugar. Beat in vanilla and eggs until light and fluffy. In a large bowl, combine flour, salt and baking soda. Gradually stir flour mixture into egg mixture until blended. Stir in chocolate pieces and nuts. Divide dough into 4 equal pieces. Shape each piece into an 8- to 10-inch roll. Wrap each roll in 1 piece of waxed paper or plastic wrap. Place wrapped rolls in a plastic freezer container with a tight-fitting lid, or wrap airtight in a 14" x 12" piece of heavy-duty foil. Label with date and contents. Store in freezer. Use within 6 months. Makes 4 rolls of dough or about 12 dozen cookies.

To bake 1 roll of dough: Preheat oven to 350°F (175°C). Cut frozen dough into 1-inch thick slices. Cut each slice into 4 equal pieces. Arrange cut pieces on an ungreased baking sheet about 1-1/2 inches apart. Bake 10 minutes until lightly browned around edges. Remove cookies from baking sheets. Cool on wire racks. Makes about 36 cookies.

Small Family Freezer Mixes

Cream Cheese Pastry Mix

Thaw the dough completely before you roll it out. It will take about four hours.

4 (3-oz.) pkgs. cream cheese, softened
1 lb. butter or margarine, softened

5 cups all-purpose flour

Cut eight 12-inch squares of plastic wrap and heavy-duty foil; set aside. In a large bowl, beat cream cheese and butter or margarine until blended. Add flour all at once. Knead in flour until evenly distributed. Shape into a large ball. Divide into 8 smaller balls. Slightly flatten each ball. Wrap each flattened ball in a piece of plastic wrap. Place 1 wrapped ball on each piece of foil. Fold foil tightly against dough, making an airtight seal. Label each package with date and contents. Store in freezer. Use within 6 months. Makes 8 packages CREAM CHEESE PASTRY MIX, enough for 8 single-crust pies, 4 double-crust pies or 80 tart shells.

Cream Cheese Pastry

To make single-crust pie: Completely thaw 1 package CREAM CHEESE PASTRY MIX. If baking empty crust, preheat oven to 450°F (230°C). On a lightly floured surface or between 2 lightly floured pieces of plastic wrap, roll out dough to an 11-inch circle. Remove plastic wrap if used. Carefully fit rolled-out dough into an 8- or 9-inch pie plate without stretching dough. Trim and flute edge. Prick crust with the tines of a fork. Bake about 10 minutes in preheated oven until lightly browned. Or add filling and bake according to filling directions. **To make double-crust pie:** Completely thaw 2 packages CREAM CHEESE PASTRY MIX. Prepare 1 ball of dough according to directions above; do not prick crust or flute edge. Turn filling into shell. Roll out top crust. Place over filling. Press edges together; flute pressed edges. Cut small slits in top crust to let steam escape. Bake according to directions for filling.

CREAM CHEESE PASTRY MIX makes:
Almond Kringle, page 137
Chess Tarts, page 135

Lime Tarts Supreme, page 134
Pecan Tarts, page 135

Meat Loaf Mix

Shape 2 cups of this mix into meatballs for a quick addition to spaghetti.

2 eggs, beaten
1 (8-oz.) can tomato sauce
2 tablespoons dried chopped onion
1 teaspoon salt
1 tablespoon Worcestershire sauce
1/4 teaspoon ground sage

1/4 teaspoon ground oregano
1/4 teaspoon ground marjoram
1/4 teaspoon celery salt
2 lbs. lean ground beef
1/2 cup breadcrumbs

In a large bowl, combine eggs, tomato sauce, onion, salt, Worcestershire sauce, sage, oregano, marjoram and celery salt. Stir in ground beef and breadcrumbs. Spoon evenly into three 2-cup freezer containers with tight-fitting lids. Attach lids. Label containers with date and contents. Store in freezer. Use within 3 months. Makes 3 packages or about 6 cups MEAT LOAF MIX.

MEAT LOAF MIX makes:
Casserole Pizza, page 130
Meat Loaf Tarts, page 132

Meat Loaf Wellington, page 132
Stuffed Porcupine Peppers, page 133

Freeze extra tomato paste by spooning mounds of tomato paste onto waxed paper. When frozen, store the frozen mounds in plastic bags.

High Health Freezer Mixes
Chili Beans & Wheat Mix

Dried oregano leaves flavor the sauce while ground oregano is absorbed and flavors the meat.

3 cups dried pinto beans
3/4 cup whole-wheat kernels
3 qts. water
2 teaspoons granulated sugar
1 teaspoon ground cumin
1 tablespoon chili powder
1 teaspoon dried oregano leaves, crushed
1/8 teaspoon dried minced garlic or
   1 garlic clove, minced
1 cup coarsely chopped onions
1 medium green pepper, chopped

1 (28-oz.) can whole tomatoes,
   slightly mashed
2 (6-oz.) cans tomato paste
2 lbs. ground beef
2 teaspoons salt
1 teaspoon ground cumin
1 tablespoon chili powder
1/2 teaspoon ground oregano
1/2 teaspoon garlic salt
1 tablespoon seasoning salt

In a large colander, wash beans and whole-wheat kernels. In a large pot or Dutch oven, combine beans, wheat and water. Soak overnight. In the morning, add sugar, 1 teaspoon cumin, 1 tablespoon chili powder, 1 teaspoon dried oregano leaves, garlic, onions, green pepper, tomatoes and tomato paste; set aside. In a large skillet, brown ground beef. Use a fork to break up meat. Drain drippings from skillet; discard drippings. Stir in salt, 1 teaspoon cumin, 1 tablespoon chili powder, 1/2 teaspoon oregano, garlic salt and seasoning salt. Simmer 2 minutes. Stir meat mixture into bean mixture. Bring to a boil over medium-high heat. Simmer over low heat, uncovered, 5 to 6 hours or until beans are tender. Cool on a rack. Ladle into eight 2-cup freezer containers with tight-fitting lids. Leave 1/2-inch air space at top of each. Cut through mixture in each container with a knife several times to remove air pockets. Attach lids. Label containers with date and contents. Store in freezer. Use within 6 months. Makes 8 packages or about 13 cups CHILI BEANS & WHEAT MIX.

CHILI BEANS & WHEAT MIX makes:
Chili Mexicano, page 144
Chili Tostadas, page 144

Mexican Pinwheels, page 144
Quick Baked Chimichangas, page 146

Whole-Wheat Pie Crust Mix

You'll be delighted with the tender, flaky crust made with this mix.

5 cups whole-wheat flour
5 cups unbleached or all-purpose flour

4 teaspoons salt
4 cups vegetable shortening

In a large bowl, combine whole-wheat flour, unbleached or all-purpose flour and salt. Stir with a wire whisk until blended. With a pastry blender or a heavy-duty mixer with a bowl cover, cut in shortening until evenly distributed. Mixture will resemble cornmeal. Spoon about 3-3/4 cups mix into each of four 4-cup freezer containers with tight-fitting lids. Attach lids. Label containers with date and contents. Store in refrigerator 10 to 12 weeks or in freezer up to 6 months. Makes 4 packages or about 15 cups WHOLE-WHEAT PIE CRUST MIX, enough to make 8 single-crust pies or 4 double-crust pies.

Whole-Wheat Pie Crust

1 pkg. WHOLE-WHEAT PIE CRUST MIX,
  thawed, see above
1 egg, beaten

1/3 cup ice water
1 tablespoon white vinegar

To make single pie crust: If baking empty crust, preheat oven to 450°F (230°C). Crumble WHOLE-WHEAT PIE CRUST MIX into a medium bowl. In a small bowl, combine egg, water and vinegar. Stir to blend. While tossing with a fork, sprinkle egg mixture over mix 1 tablespoon at a time. Continue to toss with a fork until dough clings together. Gently shape dough into 2 equal balls. On a lightly floured surface or between 2 sheets of lightly floured plastic wrap, roll out each ball to an 11-inch circle about 1/8-inch thick. Remove plastic wrap. Carefully fit rolled-out dough into an 8- or 9-inch pie plate without stretching dough. Trim and flute edge. Prick crust with the tines of a fork. Bake 10 to 15 minutes in preheated oven until lightly browned. Or add filling and bake according to filling directions. **To make double-crust pie:** Prepare according to directions above; do not prick crust or flute edge. Turn filling into shell. Roll out top crust. Place over filling. Press edges together. Trim 1/2 inch larger than pie plate; flute pressed edges. Cut small slits in top crust to let steam escape. Bake according to directions for filling.

WHOLE-WHEAT PIE CRUST MIX makes:
Deep-Dish Pot Pie, page 77
Meat & Potato Pie, page 76

Appetizers & Snacks

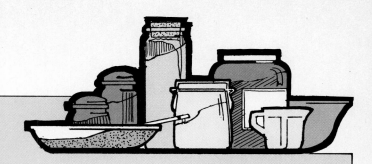

Appetizers excite or stimulate the appetite. They make a dinner party special and tantalize the imagination about what is yet to come. Historians tell us appetizers had their beginning in Russia where after long hours of travel, guests were served bits of food to satisfy them until a meal was prepared. If this is true, then the French were not far behind. Any French cookbook contains fascinating appetizers, canapés and hors d'oeuvres. Canapés are cheese, meat mixtures or a relish spread on crackers, bread or toast.

Fried appetizers should be served hot. They wilt and are not as appealing when cold. Won Tons, the ideal fried appetizer, can be served as the first course of a casual meal or of a formal dinner. Serve them hot with Sweet & Sour Sauce. Won ton skins are available in the Oriental section of your supermarket or in specialty shops. They freeze well and thaw easily.

Serve appetizers attractively, arranging tasty tidbits on small platters which can be easily replenished. Large trays soon loose their neat appearance. Vary the types of appetizers served at a buffet dinner or casual get-together. Appetizers are often finger foods and may be served either hot or cold, simple or elaborate. Offer your guests crisp vegetables stuffed with some of the cheese from Keepsake Cheese Ball.

Snacks are more substantial than appetizers. They are a light meal usually served between main meals. Thin Wheat Crackers and Holiday Cheese Ball can be served as either appetizers or snacks. They are wholesome and simple to make. You will find other appetizers and nutrition-packed snacks in High Health, pages 139 to 148.

Although most are intended as appetizers or snacks to serve a large number of people, some recipes in this section can be easily expanded into main dishes. Cheese Tortilla Stacks cut in half will serve two people. Add a fresh green salad, Cowboy Beans, page 70, and a cool drink and you have a complete meal.

Although Salty Butter Sticks are included in this section, these soft bread sticks are excellent as a bread with a full meal.

Salty Butter Sticks

These are soft, chewy and irresistible.

1/4 cup butter
2 cups SOPAIPILLA MIX, page 9
1-1/2 teaspoons baking powder

About 2/3 cup milk
Salt

Preheat oven to 450°F (230°C). Melt butter in an 8- or 9-inch square baking pan in preheating oven. Remove as soon as butter melts. In a medium bowl, combine SOPAIPILLA MIX and baking powder, stirring with a wire whisk to blend. Use a fork to stir in milk until dough forms a ball. Turn out onto a lightly floured surface; knead 8 to 10 times. Roll out dough to an 8- or 9-inch square, about 1/2 inch thick. Cut in half. Cut each half into 4'' x 1'' strips. Dip each strip in melted butter. Arrange in pan with sides touching. Sprinkle lightly with salt. Bake 15 to 20 minutes in preheated oven until golden brown. Serve hot. Makes 16 sticks.

Keepsake Cheese Ball

Spread this cheese mixture on Thin Wheat Crackers, page 55, or vegetable slices.

1 (6-oz.) jar blue cheese spread
1 (6-oz.) jar American cheese spread
1 (6-oz.) jar pimiento cheese spread
1 (8-oz.) pkg. cream cheese, softened
3 tablespoons dried parsley leaves, crushed

2 teaspoons dried minced onion
1/2 cup coarsely chopped nuts
1 tablespoon parsley leaves, crushed
1/2 cup finely chopped nuts

In a large bowl, blend cheese spreads, cream cheese, 3 tablespoons parsley, onion and 1/2 cup coarsely chopped nuts. Divide in half; shape into 2 balls. Refrigerate 4 hours or overnight. In a pie plate or shallow dish, combine 1 tablespoon parsley and 1/2 cup finely chopped nuts. Roll each cheese ball in parsley-nut mixture until surface is coated with mixture. Serve immediately or cut two 12-inch squares each of plastic wrap and heavy-duty foil. Wrap each ball separately in plastic wrap. Place 1 wrapped cheese ball in center of 1 prepared foil square. Wrap foil tightly against cheese ball to make an air-tight package. Repeat with second cheese ball. Label with date and contents. If stored in freezer, use within 6 months. If stored in refrigerator, use within 2 to 3 weeks. Makes 2 cheese balls.

Holiday Cheese Ball

Serve with Thin Wheat Crackers, page 55, or Bagels, page 106.

2 (8-oz.) pkgs. cream cheese,
  room temperature
1 (4-oz.) jar maraschino cherries,
  well-drained, finely chopped
1/3 cup finely diced green pepper

2 tablespoons dried minced onion
1 cup well-drained crushed pineapple
1/4 teaspoon seasoning salt
3/4 cup finely chopped pecans

In a large bowl, blend cream cheese, cherries, green pepper, onion, pineapple and seasoning salt. Divide in half; shape into 2 balls. Refrigerate 4 hours or overnight. Pour chopped pecans into a pie plate or shallow dish. Roll each cheese ball in nuts until surface is coated with nuts. Serve immediately or cut two 12-inch squares each of plastic wrap and heavy-duty foil. Wrap each ball separately in plastic wrap. Place 1 wrapped cheese ball in center of 1 prepared foil square. Wrap foil tightly against cheese ball to make an airtight package. Repeat with second cheese ball. Label with date and contents. If stored in freezer, use within 6 months. If stored in refrigerator, use within 2 to 3 weeks. Makes 2 cheese balls.

Keepsake Cheese Ball, Holiday Cheese Ball, Thin Wheat Crackers, page 55, and Bagels, page 106.

Cheese Crisps

Guacamole, sour cream or green chili salsa also make good toppings for cheese crisps.

10 (9-inch) Flour Tortillas, page 9   Salt & pepper to taste
3 tablespoons butter or margarine
5 cups shredded Cheddar cheese
  (1 lb. 4 oz.)

Prepare tortillas. In a large skillet, melt about 1 teaspoon butter or margarine. Add 1 tortilla. Top with 1/2 cup shredded cheese. Cook over medium heat until cheese is melted and tortilla is crisp and browned on bottom. Remove from heat; cut in 8 wedges. Sprinkle with salt and pepper to taste. Repeat process with remaining tortillas. Serve hot. Makes 80 wedges.

Cheese Fondue

With fondue this easy to make, you'll be tempted to serve it every day.

3 cups FREEZER CHEESE SAUCE MIX,   1 (1-lb.) loaf French bread,
  page 36, thawed   cut in 1-inch cubes
1/4 teaspoon dry mustard   2 red Delicious apples, sliced, if desired
Pinch garlic powder

In a medium saucepan, combine FREEZER CHEESE SAUCE MIX, dry mustard and garlic powder. Stir until heated through. Pour into a warm fondue pot. Serve with French bread cubes and apple slices, if desired. Makes 8 to 10 servings.

Cinnamon Crispies

Very light and crispy.

10 (9-inch) Flour Tortillas, page 9   1 teaspoon cinnamon
1/2 cup sugar   Oil for deep-frying

Prepare tortillas, set aside. In a small bowl, combined sugar and cinnamon; set aside. Pour oil 2 inches deep in a medium skillet, medium saucepan or mini-fryer. Heat oil to 375°F (190°C). At this temperature a 1-inch cube of bread will turn golden brown in 40 seconds. Cut each tortilla into 8 strips about 1 inch wide. Fry 3 to 5 strips at a time in hot oil until golden brown and crisp, turning once. Drain on paper towels. Sprinkle with cinnamon-sugar mixture while still warm. Serve immediately. Makes about 80 crispies.

Thin Wheat Crackers

Photo on page 53.

Roll the dough very thin so the baked crackers will be crisp.

3 cups WHOLE-WHEAT HOT ROLL MIX,   **1 cup water**
    page 33   **Salt**
5 tablespoons vegetable oil

Preheat oven to 350°F (175°C). In a medium bowl, combine WHOLE-WHEAT HOT ROLL MIX, oil and water. Stir with a fork until blended. On a lightly floured surface, knead dough only until smooth, about 3 minutes. Divide dough into 4 pieces. Roll out dough 1 piece at a time to a 16'' x 12'' rectangle, 1/16 inch thick. Place dough on an ungreased baking sheet. Use a pastry cutter or a tailor's tracing wheel to mark cutting lines on dough, drawing horizontal and diagonal lines at 2-inch intervals to make diamonds. Prick each cracker several times with tines of a fork. Sprinkle lightly with salt. Repeat with remaining dough. Bake 10 to 20 minutes in preheated oven until golden brown. Cool on a rack. Break apart at perforated lines. Makes about 200 crackers.

How to Make Thin Wheat Crackers

1/Roll dough into a thin rectangle. Cut into 2-inch diamonds. Prick with fork.

2/Cool baked crackers on a rack. Break apart at perforated lines.

Won Tons

Serve these won tons at your next buffet dinner.

Sweet & Sour Sauce, see below
1 pkg. CUBED PORK MIX, page 39,
   thawed
1/4 teaspoon freshly grated ginger

2 tablespoons finely sliced green onion
2 teaspoons soy sauce
1 (16-oz.) pkg. won ton skins
Oil for deep-frying

Sweet & Sour Sauce:
2 tablespoons cornstarch
1-1/4 cups pineapple juice
2 tablespoons white vinegar

1/3 cup packed brown sugar
1/4 cup ketchup
1 tablespoon soy sauce

Prepare Sweet & Sour Sauce; keep warm. Shred meat from CUBED PORK MIX with 2 forks. In a medium bowl, combine shredded meat, remaining mix, ginger, onion and soy sauce. Place about 1 teaspoon pork mixture in center of each won ton skin. Moisten edges with water. Bring opposite corners together to make a triangle. Seal by pressing edges firmly with your fingers. Pour oil about 2 inches deep in a deep-fryer or medium saucepan. Heat oil to 375°F (190°C). With a slotted spoon, carefully lower filled won tons into hot oil. Cook about 30 seconds on each side until crisp and golden brown. Drain on paper towels. To serve, dip won tons into sauce. Makes about 36 won tons.

Sweet & Sour Sauce:
In a medium saucepan, combine cornstarch and 1/4 cup pineapple juice until smooth. Stir in remaining ingredients. Cook and stir over medium heat until smooth and slightly thickened.

How to Make Won Tons

1/Remove meat cubes from mix. Shred meat by pulling apart with 2 forks.

2/Spoon filling onto skins. Moisten edges. Fold diagonally; pinch edges to seal.

Cheese Tortilla Stacks

One uncut stack makes two to three main-dish servings.

10 (9-inch) Flour Tortillas, page 9
2-2/3 cups shredded Monterey Jack cheese
   (9-1/2 oz.)
2-2/3 cups shredded Cheddar cheese
   (9-1/2 oz.)

2 (7-oz.) cans green chili salsa
6 thinly sliced green onions
2 (2-1/4-oz.) cans sliced pitted olives
1/4 cup butter or margarine, melted

Prepare tortillas. Preheat oven to 400°F (205°C). Lightly grease a large baking sheet. Place 1 tortilla on prepared baking sheet. Sprinkle evenly with 1/3 cup Monterey Jack cheese and 1/3 cup Cheddar cheese. Sprinkle about 2 tablespoons green chili salsa, 1 tablespoon green onions and 2 teaspoons sliced olives over cheese. Cover with another tortilla, repeating layers until 4 tortillas have been used. Top with 1 more tortilla; brush with melted butter or margarine. Make another stack with remaining 5 tortillas and remaining fillings. Bake 7 to 10 minutes in preheated oven until cheese melts and tortillas are browned. Cut in wedges. Makes 4 to 6 main dish servings or 8 to 10 snack servings.

Variation

Place tortillas in a single layer on counter. Top each with 1/3 cup Monterey Jack cheese, 1/3 cup Cheddar cheese, 2 tablespoons green chili salsa, 1 tablespoon green onions and 2 teaspoons sliced olives. Bake 3 to 5 minutes in 400°F (205°C) oven. Makes 10 servings.

Savory French Onion Loaves

Grated onion is finer than minced onion and results in a smoother spread.

1 loaf French Bread, page 103
French Onion Spread, see below

2 teaspoons dried parsley leaves, crushed
2 tablespoons grated Parmesan cheese

French Onion Spread:
1/2 cup butter or margarine
2 tablespoons Worcestershire sauce

1 cup mayonnaise
1 medium onion, grated

Prepare French Bread; cool completely. Prepare French Onion Spread; set aside. Preheat broiler, if necessary. Cut bread in half lengthwise. Cover cut surfaces with French Onion Spread. Combine parsley and cheese. Sprinkle evenly over spread. Broil 4 to 5 inches from heat source until cheese melts, 30 to 60 seconds. Cut in 2-inch slices. Serve hot. Makes 6 to 8 servings.

French Onion Spread:

In a small bowl, cream butter or margarine with Worcestershire sauce and mayonnaise. Stir in grated onion.

Soups, Sauces & Salad Dressings

Using WHITE SAUCE BUTTER-BALLS is the fastest way we know to make Basic White Sauce. When pressed for time, crumble 1, 2 or 3 of these butter-balls into any cooked vegetable and add enough milk to obtain the thickness you desire.

Expand your array of sauces by using one of the basic recipes and substituting other finely chopped or pureed vegetables, cooked meat or fish. To vary flavors, substitute canned vegetable juices, water in which vegetables have been cooked or liquid from canned vegetables in place of part of the milk in your white sauce.

Several hours before they are needed, rinse salad greens in lukewarm water. Shake off excess moisture, wrap in paper towels and store in a plastic bag or in a bowl with a tight-fitting lid. Place them in the refrigerator to chill thoroughly. To prevent edges from turning brown, tear greens into bite-size pieces instead of cutting them. Before serving, toss with enough of your favorite chilled dressing to just coat the ingredients or serve a variety of dressings and have your family or guests dress their individual salads.

Main-dish salads should combine a variety of vegetables, meats or cheese. Top them with a rich creamy dressing such as Blue Cheese Dressing. Use Roquefort, king of the blue cheeses, Danish bleu or British Stilton to add a piquant taste to this delicious dressing. After a heavy meal, there's nothing more pleasing than a dish of mixed fresh fruit dribbled with Sweet Lime Dressing.

You'll find other salad dressings among pantry and refrigerator mixes. Priscilla's Salad Dressing, page 16, adds just the right touch to a spinach salad garnished with crumbled bacon and slices of hard-cooked eggs.

Hearty Beef Chowder

Thaw all frozen meat mixtures 24 to 48 hours in the refrigerator.

1 pkg. ALL-PURPOSE GROUND BEEF
 MIX, page 37, thawed
4 cups tomato juice
1 cup water
2-1/2 cups Creamed Celery Sauce,
 page 64, or 2 (10-1/4-oz.) cans
 condensed cream of celery soup

2-1/2 cups peeled, grated carrots
1 teaspoon sugar
1/4 teaspoon garlic salt
1/4 teaspoon pepper
1/8 teaspoon ground marjoram
6 thin slices Swiss cheese

In a large saucepan, combine ALL-PURPOSE GROUND BEEF MIX, tomato juice, water and Creamed Celery Sauce or cream of celery soup. Stir with a wire whisk to blend. Stir in carrots, sugar, garlic salt, pepper and marjoram. Bring mixture to a boil over medium-high heat. Simmer 30 minutes over low heat. To serve, place 1 slice Swiss cheese in bottoms of 6 shallow soup bowls. Pour hot soup over cheese. Serve immediately. Makes 6 servings.

Grandma's Hamburger Soup

Add any leftover vegetables you have on hand.

**1 pkg. FIVE-WAY BEEF MIX made with
  hamburger, page 42, thawed**
**1 tablespoon dried green pepper flakes or
  1/4 cup chopped green pepper**
4 cups tomato juice

1/4 cup rice or barley, uncooked
1 bay leaf, crushed
1 teaspoon sugar
1 teaspoon Worcestershire sauce
Parmesan cheese for garnish

In a large saucepan or Dutch oven, combine all ingredients. Bring to a boil over medium heat. Cover; simmer 20 to 30 minutes. Ladle into 6 or 8 soup bowls. Garnish each with Parmesan cheese. Makes 6 to 8 servings.

Variation

Substitute 2 cups water for 2 cups tomato juice. Substitute 1 cup broken noodles for 1/4 cup rice or barley.

How to Make Grandma's Hamburger Soup

1/Combine mix and rice or barley with other ingredients. Simmer to blend flavors.

2/Serve piping hot, garnished with Parmesan cheese.

Best-Ever Minestrone Soup

This is our favorite soup!

1 (28-oz.) can tomatoes
1 pkg. ALL-PURPOSE GROUND BEEF
    MIX, page 37, thawed
1 qt. water
2 large carrots, peeled, sliced
2 (8-oz.) cans tomato sauce
2 cups beef broth
1 tablespoon dried parsley leaves
1/2 teaspoon basil leaves

1 teaspoon dried oregano leaves
1/4 teaspoon pepper
1/2 teaspoon garlic salt
1 (15-oz.) can garbanzo beans, drained
1 (16-oz.) can green beans, drained
1 (15-oz.) can kidney beans, drained
1-1/4 cups mostaccioli macaroni, uncooked
Parmesan cheese for garnish

Puree tomatoes in blender. In a large pot or Dutch oven, combine ALL-PURPOSE GROUND BEEF MIX, pureed tomatoes, water, carrots, tomato sauce, broth, parsley, basil, oregano, pepper and garlic salt. Bring to a boil. Cover; simmer over low heat about 20 minutes. Add garbanzo beans, green beans and kidney beans. Bring to a boil; add macaroni. Cook 15 to 20 minutes until macaroni is tender. Garnish with Parmesan cheese. Makes 10 to 12 servings.

French Onion Soup Gratiné

You'll enjoy this quick version of an international favorite.

2 pkgs. ONION SEASONING MIX,
    page 19
4 cups water or beef broth
1/4 cup butter or margarine, softened

6 slices French bread, 1 inch thick
3 cups shredded Swiss cheese (12 oz.)
2 tablespoons grated Parmesan cheese

In a large saucepan, combine ONION SEASONING MIX and water or broth. Bring to a boil over medium-high heat. Simmer over low heat about 10 minutes. Preheat oven to 375°F (190°C). Spread butter or margarine evenly on 1 side of bread slices. Arrange buttered bread slices on an ungreased baking sheet. Toast bread in oven until browned and quite dry, about 10 minutes. Remove from oven. Sprinkle about 2 tablespoons Swiss cheese on each toasted bread slice. Return bread to oven until cheese melts. Divide remaining Swiss cheese evenly in 6 soup bowls. Pour soup into bowls. Float 1 bread slice on top of each. Sprinkle evenly with Parmesan cheese. Makes 6 servings.

Creamed Mushroom Sauce

Use this blend of white sauce and mushrooms in place of condensed cream of mushroom soup.

1-1/3 cups milk
4 WHITE SAUCE BUTTER-BALLS,
  page 40
1-1/2 teaspoons instant beef
  bouillon granules

1 teaspoon Worcestershire sauce
1/2 cup finely chopped fresh mushrooms

In a small saucepan, combine milk, WHITE SAUCE BUTTER-BALLS, bouillon granules and Worcestershire sauce. Use a wire whisk to crush butter-balls. Stir constantly over medium heat until mixture is smooth and thickened. Stir in chopped mushrooms. Makes about 1-2/3 cups.

Variation
Creamed Mushroom Soup: Increase milk to 2-1/3 cups.

How to Make Creamed Mushroom Sauce

1/Use a wire whisk to break up WHITE SAUCE BUT-TER-BALLS in milk mixture.

2/Stir constantly until smooth and thickened. Stir in chopped mushrooms.

Swiss Hamburger Soup

You can change the flavor by changing the cheese to kuminost, Monterey Jack or Cheddar.

**1 pkg. FIVE-WAY BEEF MIX made with
   hamburger, page 42, thawed**
1 (16-oz.) can tomatoes

2 cups water
1 lb. Swiss cheese, cut in cubes

In a large saucepan, combine FIVE-WAY BEEF MIX, tomatoes and water. Simmer 20 to 30 minutes over low heat. Before serving, stir in cheese cubes until softened but not melted. Makes 6 to 8 servings.

Basic White Sauce

Heat and stir—that's all there is to it.

**1, 2 or 3 WHITE SAUCE BUTTER-BALLS,
   page 40**
1 cup cold milk

To make thin white sauce: In a small saucepan, combine 1 WHITE SAUCE BUTTER-BALL and milk. Use a wire whisk to crush butter-ball. Stir constantly over medium heat until mixture is smooth and slightly thickened. **To make medium white sauce:** Prepare as above using 2 WHITE SAUCE BUTTER-BALLS. **To make thick white sauce:** Prepare as above using 3 WHITE SAUCE BUTTER-BALLS. Makes about 1 cup.

Variations

A la King Sauce: Sauté 2 tablespoons finely chopped green pepper in 2 teaspoons butter or margarine. Add sautéed green pepper and 2 tablespoons chopped, canned pimiento to medium white sauce.
Creamy Rich Sauce: Substitute heavy cream for half of the milk in medium white sauce.
Onion Sauce: Sauté 1 thinly sliced large onion in 2 tablespoons melted butter or margarine. Add to medium white sauce.
Curry Sauce: Add 1 teaspoon curry powder to medium white sauce.
Herb Sauce: Add 1 tablespoon crushed dried parsley and 1-1/2 teaspoons crushed dried dill weed to medium white sauce.
Cheese Sauce: Add 1 cup shredded Cheddar cheese to medium white sauce. Stir until cheese melts; do not boil.

Creamed Celery Sauce

Use this delicious and smooth sauce in Vegetable & Cheese Casserole, page 74.

3 tablespoons water
1/2 cup finely chopped celery
1-1/3 cups milk
4 WHITE SAUCE BUTTER-BALLS,
  page 40

1-1/2 teaspoons instant
  vegetarian bouillon granules

In a small saucepan, combine water and celery. Cover; cook over medium heat until celery is tender, about 4 minutes. Drain if necessary; set aside. In same small saucepan, combine milk, WHITE SAUCE BUTTER-BALLS and bouillon granules. Use a wire whisk to crush butter-balls. Stir constantly over medium heat until mixture is smooth and thickened. Stir in cooked celery. Makes about 1-2/3 cups.

Variation

Creamed Celery Soup: Increase milk to 2-1/3 cups.

Creamed Chicken Sauce

Chopped turkey or ham can be substituted for the chopped chicken.

1-1/3 cups milk
4 WHITE SAUCE BUTTER-BALLS,
  page 40
1/4 teaspoon ground tarragon
1/4 teaspoon celery salt

1/4 teaspoon onion powder
1-1/2 teaspoons instant chicken
  bouillon granules
1/2 cup finely chopped chicken

In a small saucepan, combine milk, WHITE SAUCE BUTTER-BALLS, tarragon, celery salt, onion powder and bouillon granules. Use a wire whisk to crush butter-balls. Stir constantly over medium heat until mixture is smooth and thickened. Stir in chicken. Makes about 1-2/3 cups.

Variation

Creamed Chicken Soup: Increase milk to 2-1/3 cups.

Sweet Lime Dressing

Try this bitter-sweet combination on fresh fruit.

1 cup CHEF'S SALAD DRESSING MIX,
  page 28
3 tablespoons honey

2 tablespoons lime juice
1 teaspoon celery seeds
1/4 teaspoon paprika

In a small bowl, combine all ingredients. Stir to mix well. Refrigerate 30 minutes before serving. Makes about 1-1/4 cups.

Blue Cheese Dressing

Crumble blue cheese by pulling it apart with two forks.

1 cup CHEF'S SALAD DRESSING MIX,
  page 28

1/4 cup crumbled Roquefort or
  other blue cheese (1 oz.)

In a small bowl, combine CHEF'S SALAD DRESSING MIX and blue cheese. Refrigerate 30 minutes before serving. Makes about 1-1/4 cups.

Thousand Island Dressing

It takes only seconds to make this dressing.

1 cup CHEF'S SALAD DRESSING MIX,
  page 28
1/4 cup chili sauce

2 hard-cooked eggs, chopped, if desired
1 tablespoon chopped sweet pickle

In a small bowl, combine all ingredients. Stir to mix well. Refrigerate 30 minutes before serving. Makes about 1-1/4 cups.

Vegetables & Side Dishes

Vegetables are at their best when freshly picked. Use your home-grown vegetables if possible or purchase them close to the time of preparation. Buy perishable fresh vegetables in season when prices are reasonable. Damaged vegetables are not a bargain. As you shop for vegetables for Old-Fashioned Vegetable Platter, buy those that are young, fresh and free from bruises, skin punctures and decay. Use the Vegetable Buying Guide to the right.

Old-Fashioned Vegetable Platter can be served as a side dish or main dish. FREEZER CHEESE SAUCE MIX, page 36, adds the necessary protein to make it a complete meal.

Most vegetables are enhanced by adding a cheese sauce. If you don't have FREEZER CHEESE SAUCE MIX on hand, use the cheese-sauce variation of Basic White Sauce, page 63.

Those who like Italian cooking will enjoy Eggplant Parmesan and Green Peppers Italian-Style. Both are made with ITALIAN-STYLE MEAT MIX, page 38.

Vegetable Buying Guide

Asparagus	Firm, closed, compact tips; smooth, crisp, tender spears
Broccoli	Firm, compact cluster of dark green buds with no yellow flowers; slim stems
Brussels sprouts	Tight-fitting outer leaves; firm body free from blemishes
Cabbage	Firm heavy heads; outer leaves rich green or red; crisp, free from blemishes
Carrots	Medium to small; bright-colored; firm
Cauliflower	Head white to creamy-white; compact
Corn	Silk ends free from decay or worm damage; kernels plump but tender
Lettuce, iceberg	Large, round, solid heads; medium green outer leaves; pale green inner leaves
Lettuce, leaf	Broad, tender, juicy leaves; smooth; pale green to deep green
Mushrooms	Young; small to medium; caps closed tightly around stems or slightly opened; tops of caps white or creamy
Peppers, green	Firm, glossy walls, medium to dark green; moderate to heavy for size
Potatoes	Uniform shape; firm; free from blemishes & green sunburn
Squash, summer	Tender, glossy skin; firm but not hard
Tomatoes	Uniform shape; evenly red; tender, firm

Green Peppers Italian-Style

For exceptional flavor, use 1/2 pound fresh mushrooms in this delightful side dish.

3 tablespoons vegetable oil
4 large green peppers, cut in thin strips
1/2 teaspoon onion salt
1/4 teaspoon pepper

2 (4-oz.) cans mushrooms, drained
1/2 cup ITALIAN-STYLE MEAT MIX, page 38

Heat oil in a large skillet. Add green pepper strips, onion salt and pepper. Stirring occasionally, sauté over medium-high heat until peppers are crisp-tender, about 3 minutes. Stir in mushrooms and ITALIAN-STYLE MEAT MIX. Simmer over low heat until heated through, 15 to 20 minutes. Makes 6 to 8 servings.

Marinated Bean Salad   Photo on page 30.

Going on a picnic? Prepare this tangy bean salad the night before.

1 (16-oz.) can cut green beans, drained
1 (16-oz.) can cut wax beans, drained
1 (15-oz.) can garbanzo beans, drained
1 (15-oz.) can red kidney beans, drained
1 medium red onion, thinly sliced,
  separated in rings

1 medium green pepper, sliced in rings
1/3 cup sugar
1-1/2 cups MARINADE BLEND MIX,
  page 31

In a large bowl, combine all ingredients, stirring gently to evenly distribute MARINADE BLEND MIX. Cover; refrigerate 3 hours or overnight. Makes about 8 servings.

Italian-Style Zucchini

You'll impress your guests with this new side dish.

4 or 5 medium zucchini
2 tablespoons vegetable oil
1 medium onion, sliced, separated in rings
1/4 teaspoon salt

1/8 teaspoon pepper
1-1/2 cups ITALIAN-STYLE MEAT MIX,
  page 38, thawed

Cut zucchini in 1/4-inch slices. Heat oil in a large saucepan. Add onion rings, salt and pepper. Stirring occasionally, simmer over medium heat until lightly browned, 3 to 4 minutes. Add zucchini slices and ITALIAN-STYLE MEAT MIX. Cover; simmer over low heat until zucchini are crisp-tender, about 5 minutes. Serve immediately. Makes about 4 servings.

Creamed Peas

Substitute any fresh or frozen vegetable for the frozen peas.

1/2 cup water
1 (10-oz.) pkg. frozen peas or
  1-1/2 cups fresh peas
1/2 cup milk

2 WHITE SAUCE BUTTER-BALLS,
  page 40
3 parsley sprigs for garnish

In a medium saucepan, bring water to a boil. Add peas. Bring water to a boil again. Cover; cook over medium heat until tender. Stir in milk. Crumble WHITE SAUCE BUTTER-BALLS into mixture. Cook and stir gently until mixture becomes smooth and slightly thickened. Garnish with parsley sprigs. Makes 4 to 6 servings.

Glorified Baked Potatoes

Baked potatoes are softer and smoother when you press and roll them before they are cut.

4 large baking potatoes
1 cup SOUR CREAM & CHEESE MIX,
  page 29

2 slices bacon, cooked, crumbled

Preheat oven to 400°F (205°C). Scrub potatoes with a vegetable brush. Pierce each potato several times with tines of a fork. Bake about 1 hour in preheated oven until tender. Place baked potatoes on a firm surface. Cover with a cloth to protect your hands. Press and roll each potato to soften. Make a criss-cross cut on potato. With cut-side up, squeeze from both ends toward the middle until potato pops up through opening. Spoon about 1/4 cup SOUR CREAM & CHEESE MIX on each potato. Sprinkle tops evenly with crumbled bacon. Bake 5 minutes longer. Serve immediately. Makes 4 servings.

Tangy Cauliflower

Cook vegetables until they are just crisp-tender, not soft.

1 medium cauliflower head
1 cup SOUR CREAM & CHEESE MIX,
  page 29
1 teaspoon prepared mustard

1 medium tomato, cut in wedges,
  for garnish
Parsley sprigs for garnish

Place cauliflower head in a medium saucepan. Pour water 1/2 inch deep in saucepan; cover. Cook over medium heat until crisp-tender, 20 to 30 minutes; drain. Preheat broiler, if necessary. Place cauliflower in a 9-inch square baking dish. Set aside; keep warm. In a small bowl, combine SOUR CREAM & CHEESE MIX and mustard. Spread mixture over top and about half way down side of cooked cauliflower head. Broil until cheese is melted, about 2 minutes. Use a large spatula to lift broiled cauliflower head from baking dish to a small platter. Garnish with tomato wedges and parsley sprigs. Makes 6 to 8 servings.

Marinated Mushrooms

Buy firm, white mushrooms with tops tight against the stems.

1 lb. fresh mushrooms
1 cup MARINADE BLEND MIX, page 31

Rinse mushrooms; peel, if desired. Pat dry with paper towels. In a medium bowl, pour MARINADE BLEND MIX over mushrooms. Marinate in refrigerator at least 4 hours. Makes 6 to 8 appetizer servings.

Cauliflower Fritters in Cheese Sauce

Fresh green beans or spinach are also excellent dipped in this batter, then fried.

1 medium cauliflower head
1/2 teaspoon salt
1 pkg. FREEZER CHEESE SAUCE
MIX, page 36, thawed

3 eggs, separated
1/4 teaspoon salt
Vegetable oil for frying

Break or cut cauliflower into flowerets. In a medium saucepan, cover flowerets with water. Add 1/2 teaspoon salt. Cook uncovered over medium heat until crisp-tender, about 15 minutes. Remove from heat; drain well. In a small saucepan, heat FREEZER CHEESE SAUCE MIX over medium-low heat. Do not boil. Keep warm. In a large bowl, beat egg whites until stiff; set aside. In a medium bowl, beat egg yolks until thick. Beat in 1/4 teaspoon salt. Fold beaten egg yolk mixture into beaten egg whites; set aside. Pour oil about 3/4 inch deep in a medium skillet. Heat to 375°F (190°C). At this temperature a 1-inch cube of bread will turn golden brown in 40 seconds. Dip slightly cooled cauliflowerets into egg mixture, turning with a fork to coat all sides. Use a slotted spoon or 2 forks to carefully lower flowerets into hot oil. Cook 4 or 5 pieces at a time, turning until browned on all sides, about 1 minute. Drain on paper towels. Arrange on a platter. Drizzle warmed FREEZER CHEESE SAUCE MIX over cooked cauliflowerets. Serve immediately. Makes 6 servings.

How to Make Cauliflower Fritters in Cheese Sauce

1/Rinse cauliflower and cut or break into flowerets.

2/Dip flowerets in egg batter. Fry in hot oil until golden brown. Drain on paper towels.

Old-Fashioned Vegetable Platter

Zucchini, cocozelle, pattypan, crookneck *and* straightneck *are all summer squash.*

1 lb. broccoli	1/2 lb. fresh mushrooms
1 medium cauliflower	2 ears of corn, husked
1/4 teaspoon salt	Salt and pepper to taste
1/4 lb. brussels sprouts, if desired	1-1/2 cups FREEZER CHEESE SAUCE
4 large carrots	MIX, page 36, thawed
1/2 lb. summer squash	

Cut broccoli and cauliflower into flowerets. In a large bowl, cover flowerets with water. Stir in 1/4 teaspoon salt; set aside. Cut stem ends and damaged outer leaves from brussels sprouts. Rinse; set aside. Scrub carrots with a brush or use a peeler to remove peel. Cut in 1/4-inch slices; set aside. Rinse summer squash. Cut off blossom and stem ends. Cut in 1/2-inch slices; set aside. Rinse mushrooms. Peel, if desired; set aside. Rinse corn. Break ears of corn in half; set aside. Pour water about 1-1/2 inches deep in a large pot or Dutch oven. Insert steamer basket. Drain soaked broccoli and cauliflower; discard water. Rinse under cold running water. Place broccoli, cauliflower, brussels sprouts, carrots and squash in steamer basket. Cover pot or Dutch oven; bring water to a boil. Steam 15 minutes over medium-low heat. Add prepared mushrooms and corn. Steam 10 minutes longer until vegetables are crisp-tender. In a small saucepan, warm FREEZER CHEESE SAUCE MIX over low heat; do not boil. Arrange cooked vegetables on a large platter. Season to taste with salt and pepper. Top with warmed cheese sauce. Makes 3 or 4 main-dish servings or 6 side-dish servings.

Variation

Sprinkle 2 tablespoons finely grated Parmesan cheese or CRISP COATING MIX, page 19, evenly over top of vegetables.

Cowboy Beans

Never add baking soda when you cook beans. It destroys thiamin, a B-vitamin in beans.

3 cups dry pinto beans, rinsed	1 medium onion, finely chopped
2 qts. cold water	1 pkg. ONION SEASONING MIX,
4 cups water	page 19
2 teaspoons salt	8 slices bacon, cut in 1-inch pieces
1/8 teaspoon pepper	
1/8 teaspoon dried minced garlic or	
1 garlic clove, minced	

In a large pot or Dutch oven, combine beans and 2 quarts cold water. Bring to a boil over medium-high heat. Boil 2 minutes. Remove from heat; cover. Let stand 2 hours. Drain; discard water. Combine soaked beans, 4 cups water, salt, pepper, garlic, onion, ONION SEASONING MIX and bacon. Bring to a boil. Cover; simmer over low heat about 2 hours or until beans are tender. Makes 6 to 8 servings.

Pork Noodles

Linguine is also known as flat spaghetti.

1-1/2 cups water
1-1/2 teaspoons instant chicken
   bouillon granules
1 pkg. CUBED PORK MIX, page 39,
   thawed

1-1/2 teaspoons soy sauce
1 (8-oz.) pkg. linguine
3 hard-cooked eggs, sliced, for garnish
3 chopped green onions for garnish

In a medium saucepan, bring water to a boil. Add bouillon granules; stir until dissolved. Stir in CUBED PORK MIX and soy sauce. Bring to a boil. Simmer about 5 minutes over low heat, stirring occasionally. Cook linguine according to package directions. Spoon cooked linguine evenly into 4 soup bowls. Pour pork mixture evenly over top of each. Garnish each with hard-cooked egg slices and chopped green onions. Makes 4 servings.

Creamed Mushrooms in Toast Cups

Day-old bread will hold its shape better than fresh bread.

Crisp Toast Cups, see below
3 tablespoons butter or margarine
2 tablespoons chopped green onion
1/2 lb. fresh mushrooms, sliced
1-1/2 cups cold milk
3 WHITE SAUCE BUTTER-BALLS,
   page 40

2 teaspoons soy sauce
2 teaspoons chopped pimiento
1/4 teaspoon paprika
Parsley sprigs for garnish

Crisp Toast Cups:
12 thin slices day-old white bread
6 tablespoons butter or margarine, melted

Prepare Crisp Toast Cups; set aside. In a medium skillet, melt butter or margarine. Add green onion and mushrooms. Sauté over medium heat until tender. Remove from heat; set aside. In a medium saucepan, combine milk and WHITE SAUCE BUTTER-BALLS. Using a wire whip, crush butter-balls slightly. Stir constantly over medium heat until mixture is smooth and slightly thickened. Stir in soy sauce, chopped pimiento and mushroom mixture. Cook and stir 1 minute longer. Serve in Crisp Toast Cups. Sprinkle evenly with paprika. Garnish with parsley sprigs. Makes 6 servings.

Crisp Toast Cups:
Preheat oven to 375°F (190°C). Cut crusts from bread. Reserve crusts for another use. Carefully press trimmed bread slices into ungreased muffin cups. Brush bread with melted butter or margarine. Bake 10 to 12 minutes in preheated oven until lightly browned. Cool on a rack. Remove from muffin cups when cool.

Casseroles & Supper Dishes

ALL-PURPOSE GROUND BEEF MIX, page 37, CUBED PORK MIX, page 39, ITALIAN-STYLE MEAT MIX, page 38, FIVE-WAY BEEF MIX, page 42, and CUBED BEEF MIX, page 37, are all used in this section. These meat mixes dramatically reduce meal preparation and cleanup time. Be sure they are taken out of the freezer in time for proper thawing. If you must thaw something quickly, a microwave oven is your most convenient helper. If one is not available, thaw frozen mixes over warm water. Or thaw frozen mixes in heavy saucepans containing small amounts of water. Place over low heat, adding small amounts of water as needed.

Mixes using cubed meat call for less-tender cuts which are usually cooked by braising or moist heat. Ask your butcher for these or other cuts of meat suitable for this type of preparation. When you buy ground beef for use in mixes, lean or extra-lean will give you the best results. Regular ground beef is higher in fat content and may retain the taste and flavor of the fat. Ground hamburger mixes are excellent in chili, spaghetti sauce, meatloaf, stew and casseroles.

Convenience cooking with mixes would not be complete without stir-frying. A wok is the ideal cooking utensil, but you can use a heavy skillet. Prepare all ingredients before heating the oil because there isn't time once you begin cooking. Meat cooks faster and more uniformly if cut in thin strips 3 to 4 inches long. Vegetables cooked by stir-frying can be quickly removed from the heat by pulling them up on the sides of the wok. Nothing is more appetizing than tender, juicy, golden brown strips of meat and brightly colored vegetables cook crisp-tender so their true flavor is released and texture is maintained. Stir-Fry Cashew Chicken and Oriental Shrimp & Vegetable Stir-Fry use this cooking method.

Dinner in-a-Pumpkin

For a Halloween treat, paint a face on the pumpkin with acrylic paints before it is baked.

1 medium pumpkin
2 pkgs. ALL-PURPOSE GROUND BEEF
  MIX, page 37, thawed
1/4 cup soy sauce
2 tablespoons packed brown sugar

1 (4-oz.) can sliced mushrooms, drained
1-1/4 cups Creamed Chicken Sauce,
  page 64, or 1 (10-1/2-oz.) can condensed
  cream of chicken soup
2 cups hot cooked rice

Preheat oven to 375°F (190°C). Lightly grease a 10-inch circle in center of a baking sheet; set aside. Place pumpkin on a firm surface. Using a sharp knife, cut out stem end and about 3 inches around stem. Cut on a diagonal by slanting knife from outer edge of pumpkin toward center. Reserve top of pumpkin. Remove seeds and pulp; discard. In a medium bowl, combine ALL-PURPOSE GROUND BEEF MIX, soy sauce, brown sugar, mushrooms, sauce or soup and rice. Spoon mixture into pumpkin. Replace top of pumpkin. Place filled pumpkin on greased center of baking sheet. Bake about 1 hour in preheated oven until pumpkin is tender. To serve, spoon some of cooked pumpkin and meat filling onto plates. Makes 6 to 8 servings.

Mexican Delight

This Southwest combination will be a favorite at your next buffet dinner.

1 (30-oz.) can refried beans
1 pkg. ALL-PURPOSE GROUND BEEF
  MIX, page 37, thawed
1 (4-oz.) can diced or
  chopped green chilies
3 cups shredded Monterey Jack cheese
  (12 oz.)

1 (7-oz.) can green chili salsa
1 large ripe avocado, peeled, pitted,
  mashed, or 1 (7-3/4-oz.) pkg.
  frozen avocado dip, thawed
1 cup dairy sour cream
1 cup pitted ripe olives for garnish
1 (10-oz.) pkg. corn chips

Preheat oven to 400°F (205°C). Lightly butter a 13" x 9" baking dish. Spread refried beans in bottom of dish. Spread ALL-PURPOSE GROUND BEEF MIX evenly over beans. Sprinkle chilies evenly over meat mixture. Sprinkle with shredded cheese. Drizzle green chili salsa over cheese. Bake about 30 minutes in preheated oven until hot and bubbly. Remove from oven. Spoon mashed avocado or avocado dip in center of casserole. Spoon sour cream in a circle around avocado. Arrange olives on sour cream and avocado. Tuck about 1/3 of the corn chips around edge of dish with points up. Serve with remaining corn chips. Makes 6 servings.

Vegetable & Cheese Casserole

Serve this colorful casserole with hot Light & Tender Biscuits, page 138.

3 tablespoons butter or margarine
1 cup dry breadcrumbs
1 pkg. FIVE-WAY BEEF MIX made with
  hamburger, page 42, thawed
1 cup shredded Cheddar cheese or
  Monterey Jack cheese (4 oz.)

1-1/4 cups Creamed Celery Sauce, page 64,
  or 1 (10-1/2-oz.) can condensed
  cream of celery soup

Preheat oven to 350°F (175°C). In a small skillet, melt butter or margarine over medium-low heat. Stir in breadcrumbs. Cook and stir until crumbs are crisp and golden brown. Butter a 2-1/2 quart casserole dish. Add FIVE-WAY BEEF MIX, cheese and sauce or soup. Stir gently to combine. Top casserole with browned crumbs. Bake 30 minutes. Makes 4 to 6 servings.

Beef Ragout

Fry or microwave the bacon to remove most of the fat, if desired.

3 slices bacon, cut in 2-inch pieces
1 pkg. CUBED BEEF MIX,
  page 37, thawed
1 small to medium onion, thinly sliced

4 medium potatoes, thinly sliced
4 medium carrots, thinly sliced
Salt and pepper to taste
3/4 cup cold water

Preheat oven to 375°F (190°C). In a shallow 2-1/2-quart casserole dish, layer bacon pieces, CUBED BEEF MIX, onion slices, potato slices and carrot slices. Sprinkle with salt and pepper to taste. Gently stir in water. Cover; bake 60 to 70 minutes in preheated oven until vegetables are crisp-tender. Makes 6 servings.

Company Casserole

Introduce variety by using mostaccioli, rotini spirals *or* wheels *rather than flat noodles.*

1 pkg. ALL-PURPOSE GROUND BEEF MIX, page 37, thawed	1 (3-oz.) pkg. cream cheese, softened
1 tablespoon sugar	1/4 to 1/2 cup milk
1/2 teaspoon garlic salt	1 cup dairy sour cream
2 (8-oz.) cans tomato sauce	6 green onions, finely sliced
2 to 3 tablespoons water, if needed	1 (8-oz.) pkg. noodles, cooked, drained
	2 cups shredded Cheddar cheese (8 oz.)

Preheat oven to 350°F (175°C). Lightly butter a 2-quart casserole dish; set aside. In a medium saucepan, combine ALL-PURPOSE GROUND BEEF MIX, sugar, garlic salt and tomato sauce. Simmer over medium heat about 10 minutes. Add water if needed to keep mixture moist. In a small bowl, combine cream cheese, 1/4 cup milk and sour cream, stirring until smooth. Stir in additional milk if needed to make a medium-thick sauce. Stir in green onions. In prepared casserole dish, layer 1/2 of the cooked noodles, 1/2 of the meat mixture and 1/2 of the sour cream mixture. Repeat layers. Top evenly with shredded cheese. Bake 30 minutes in preheated oven until layers are heated through and cheese melts. Makes 6 to 8 servings.

Eggplant Parmesan

Refrigerate the casserole overnight, then bake it about 45 minutes at 375° (190°C).

Oil for frying	2-1/2 cups ITALIAN-STYLE MEAT MIX, page 38, thawed
1 medium eggplant, unpeeled	1/2 cup freshly grated Parmesan or Romano cheese
2 eggs, slightly beaten	
2 tablespoons cold water	
1-1/2 cups fine breadcrumbs	2 (6-oz.) pkgs. sliced mozzarella cheese

Pour oil for frying 1/2 inch deep in a large skillet. Heat to 365°F (185°C). At this temperature, a 1-inch cube of bread will turn golden-brown in 50 seconds. Cut eggplant into 15 slices about 1/4 inch thick; set aside. In a small shallow dish or pie plate, beat eggs and water to combine; set aside. Pour breadcrumbs into another small shallow dish or pie plate. Dip eggplant into egg mixture, then into breadcrumbs. Turning once, brown coated eggplant slices in hot oil until tender when pierced with a fork. Add more oil, if needed. Preheat oven to 375°F (190°C). Butter a 2-quart casserole dish. Arrange 5 eggplant slices over bottom of dish, overlapping if necessary. Top evenly with about 1/3 of the ITALIAN-STYLE MEAT MIX, 1/3 of the grated Parmesan or Romano cheese and 1/3 of the mozzarella cheese slices. Repeat, making 2 more layers. Bake uncovered 30 to 40 minutes until cheese melts and sauce bubbles. Makes 6 servings.

Meat & Potato Pie

Serve this family favorite with ketchup or chili sauce.

Double Freezer Pie Crust, unbaked,
   page 41, or
Double Whole-Wheat Pie Crust,
   unbaked, page 50
1 lb. lean ground beef
1/2 cup milk

1 pkg. ONION SEASONING MIX,
   page 19
1/8 teaspoon pepper
1 (12-oz.) pkg. hash brown potatoes,
   thawed, or 4 cups grated,
   cooked potatoes

Prepare bottom crust in a 9-inch pie plate; set aside. Preheat oven to 350°F (175°C). In a medium bowl, combine ground beef, milk, ONION SEASONING MIX and pepper. Press into pastry lined pie plate. Top with potatoes. Cover with top crust. Trim and flute edges. Cut slits in top crust to let steam escape. Bake 1 hour until crust is golden brown. Makes 6 servings.

Spanish Cheese Pie

You can tell if the filling is set by shaking the pie with gentle back and forth motions.

Single Freezer Pie Crust, unbaked,
   page 41
1-1/2 cups shredded Monterey Jack cheese
   (6 oz.)
1 (4-oz.) can diced or
   chopped green chilies

1 cup shredded Cheddar cheese (4 oz.)
4 eggs
1-1/2 cups half and half
1/4 teaspoon salt
1/8 teaspoon ground cumin

Prepare pie crust in a 9-inch pie plate; set aside. Preheat oven to 350°F (175°C). Sprinkle Monterey Jack cheese in bottom of unbaked pie crust. Top evenly with green chilies and 1/2 cup Cheddar cheese. In a medium bowl, beat eggs thoroughly. Stir in half and half, salt and cumin. Pour over cheese in pie crust. Top with remaining 1/2 cup Cheddar cheese. Bake 40 to 60 minutes until set. Makes 4 to 6 servings.

Turkey Dinner Pie

Simple, but special!

Double Freezer Pie Crust, unbaked,
   page 41
2-1/2 cups cooked turkey or chicken,
   cut in 1/2-inch cubes
2 cups Chicken Gravy, page 28, or
   leftover turkey gravy

1 (10-oz.) pkg. frozen carrots and peas,
   thawed
1 (8-oz.) can onions, halved
1 teaspoon salt
1/8 teaspoon pepper
1/8 teaspoon ground thyme

Prepare bottom crust in a 9-inch pie plate. Preheat oven to 425°F (220°C). In a large bowl, combine turkey or chicken, gravy, carrots and peas, onions, salt, pepper and thyme. Stir to distribute evenly. Pour into pastry shell. Cover with top crust. Trim and flute edges. Cut slits in top crust to let steam escape. Bake 35 to 40 minutes in preheated oven until golden brown. Makes 6 servings.

Deep-Dish Pot Pie

To bake the pie immediately, follow the instructions for baking given below.

**1 pkg. FIVE-WAY BEEF MIX with
   hamburger, page 42, thawed**
**Single Whole-Wheat Pie Crust, unbaked,
   page 50, or Single Freezer Pie Crust,
   unbaked, page 41**

1 egg
1 tablespoon vegetable oil

Turn FIVE-WAY BEEF MIX into an 8- or 9-inch square baking dish or a 2-1/2-quart casserole dish. Roll out pastry to a 10-inch square or to fit casserole dish. Place pastry over dish. Trim, letting dough extend 1/2 inch beyond edge of dish. Fold under edge; flute. To freeze unbaked pie, wrap airtight in heavy-duty freezer wrap or heavy-duty foil. Store in freezer. Use within 6 months. To bake frozen pie, thaw in refrigerator about 24 hours. Preheat oven to 425°F (220°C). Cut slits in crust to let steam escape. In a small bowl, beat egg and oil with a fork or a wire whisk. Brush evenly on crust with a pastry brush, covering entire crust. Bake 35 to 45 minutes in preheated oven until deep golden brown. Makes 4 to 6 servings.

Quick Pepper Beef Cubes

For a spicier flavor, increase the ginger to 1-1/2 teaspoons.

2 tablespoons vegetable oil
1 medium garlic clove, minced
**2 large green peppers,
   cut in julienne strips**
1 small onion, sliced
**1 pkg. CUBED BEEF MIX,
   page 37, thawed**

3/4 cup beef broth
3/4 teaspoon ginger
1 teaspoon sugar
6 slices bread, toasted
3 tomatoes, cut in wedges

In a large skillet, heat oil. Add garlic, green pepper strips and onion slices. Sauté over low heat until tender, 3 to 4 minutes. Stir in CUBED BEEF MIX, beef broth, ginger and sugar. Simmer over medium heat 10 minutes. Cut each piece of toast from corner to corner to make 4 toast triangles. Reserve about 7 triangles. Arrange remaining toast triangles on a small serving plate; set aside. Gently stir tomato wedges into meat mixture. Immediately turn meat mixture into a large serving bowl. Insert reserved toast triangles around edge of bowl with points up. Serve immediately with remaining toast triangles. Makes 4 to 6 servings.

Bread Basket Stew

Believe it or not, the Bread Basket Bowls hold their shape until you start to eat them.

Bread Basket Bowls, see below
1 pkg. FIVE-WAY BEEF MIX made with
   cubed beef, page 42, thawed
2 (8-oz.) cans tomato sauce
1 (17-oz.) can whole-kernel corn, undrained

2 cups sliced fresh mushrooms or
   1 (8-oz.) can mushroom pieces, drained
1 tablespoon Worcestershire sauce
1 bay leaf, if desired

Bread Basket Bowls:
1 pkg. active dry yeast (1 tablespoon)
1-1/2 cups lukewarm water (110°F, 45°C)
1 egg, slightly beaten
2 tablespoons vegetable oil

About 5-1/2 cups WHOLE-WHEAT
   HOT ROLL MIX, page 33
1 egg
1 tablespoon water

Prepare Bread Basket Bowls; set aside. In a medium saucepan, combine FIVE-WAY BEEF MIX, tomato sauce, corn, mushrooms, Worcestershire sauce and bay leaf, if desired. Bring to a boil over medium-high heat. Cover and simmer over low heat 25 minutes. Remove bay leaf. Place each Bread Basket Bowl on a plate. Ladle stew into bowls. Makes 6 to 8 servings.

Bread Basket Bowls:
In a large bowl, dissolve yeast in lukewarm water. When yeast bubbles, stir in 1 beaten egg and oil. Gradually stir in 3 cups WHOLE-WHEAT HOT ROLL MIX until blended. Add enough additional WHOLE-WHEAT HOT ROLL MIX to make a stiff dough. Turn out on a lightly floured surface. Knead until smooth, about 10 minutes. Add additional flour to surface as needed. Clean and grease bowl. Place dough in greased bowl, turning to grease all sides. Cover and let rise in a warm place until doubled in bulk, about 1-1/2 hours. While dough is rising, generously grease the outsides and bottoms of eight 10-ounce custard cups; set aside. Punch down dough. Turn out on lightly floured surface. Knead about 5 times. Divide dough into 8 equal pieces. Shape pieces of dough into smooth balls. Use a rolling pin to roll out 1 ball into a 6-inch circle. Lay rolled-out dough over 1 inverted and greased custard cup. Mold dough circle to cover cup. Repeat with other balls of dough. Arrange dough-covered custard cups on 2 ungreased baking sheets, about 2 inches apart. Let stand uncovered 10 minutes. Preheat oven to 375°F (190°C). Bake bowls 20 minutes. Beat 1 egg with 1 tablespoon water. Remove custard cups from oven. Brush bread bowls with egg-water mixture. Bake 5 minutes longer. Remove from oven. Turn right side up; remove custard cups. Brush inside of each bread bowl with egg-water mixture. Bake 10 to 15 minutes longer until lightly browned inside and outside. Cool on a wire rack.

Stir-Fry Cashew Chicken

Entertain your guests with this Oriental dish.

3 chicken breast halves, skinned, boned
About 1/3 cup vegetable oil
1 lb. fresh green beans,
 cut in 1-inch pieces
1 yam, cut in 1/4-inch slices
1 (8-oz.) can water chestnuts,
 drained, sliced

1-1/2 cups ORIENTAL STIR-FRY MIX,
 page 32
1 (3-oz.pkg.) cashew nuts
1 to 2 tablespoons water, if needed
3 cups hot cooked rice

Cut chicken into thin strips; set aside. In a large skillet or wok, heat 2 to 3 tablespoons oil. Add chicken. Stir constantly over medium heat until meat is tender, 4 to 5 minutes. Drain chicken on paper towels; cover and keep warm. Add 2 to 3 tablespoons of the remaining oil to skillet or wok. Add green beans. Cook and stir about 3 minutes. Add yam pieces. Cook and stir until beans are crisp-tender, 3 to 4 minutes. Add cooked chicken, water chestnuts and ORIENTAL STIR-FRY MIX. Cook and stir until sauce is slightly thickened, about 10 minutes. Stir in nuts and water, if needed to make a thinner sauce. Simmer 2 minutes longer. Serve over hot cooked rice. Makes 4 to 6 servings.

Slumgullion

Serve this quick combination on a day when time is short.

1 pkg. ALL-PURPOSE GROUND BEEF
 MIX, page 37, thawed
1 (12-oz.) can whole-kernel corn

2 (8-oz.) cans tomato sauce
1 (6-oz.) pkg. noodles, cooked, drained

In a medium skillet, combine ALL-PURPOSE GROUND BEEF MIX, corn and tomato sauce. Stirring occasionally, simmer over medium heat about 15 minutes. Stir hot cooked noodles into meat mixture. Simmer 10 minutes. Makes 6 servings.

Variation

Stir 2 tablespoons butter or margarine and 1/2 teaspoon dried parsley leaves into hot cooked noodles. To serve, spoon noodles onto 6 plates. Spoon meat mixture over noodles.

If beaten eggs are to be combined with a hot mixture, stir about 1/2 cup hot mixture into the beaten eggs before adding the eggs to the remaining hot mixture. This keeps the eggs from cooking into hard lumps.

Hurry-Up Curry

Curry is a blend of spices, mild to quite hot in flavor.

1 pkg. ALL-PURPOSE GROUND BEEF
   MIX, page 37,
   or 1 pkg. CUBED PORK MIX,
   page 39, thawed
1/3 cup ketchup
3/4 cup water

1 cup sliced fresh mushrooms
1 teaspoon curry powder
2 teaspoons steak sauce
2 teaspoons Worcestershire sauce
3/4 cup chutney, if desired
3 cups hot cooked rice

In a large skillet, combine ALL-PURPOSE GROUND BEEF MIX or CUBED PORK MIX, ketchup, water, mushrooms, curry powder, steak sauce and Worcestershire sauce. Stirring occasionally, cook over medium heat until heated through, about 10 minutes. If desired, spoon chutney into a small bowl. Serve curry mixture over hot cooked rice. Makes about 6 servings.

Ring-Around-the-Tuna

If you don't have a ring mold, serve the rice mixture in a bowl.

Rice Ring, see below
2 tablespoons butter or margarine
1/2 cup finely chopped onion
1/2 cup finely chopped celery
3 WHITE SAUCE BUTTER-BALLS,
   page 40

2 cups milk
2 egg yolks
1 (13-oz.) can tuna, drained
1 (4-oz.) can sliced mushrooms, drained
1 (2-oz.) jar pimiento, diced

Rice Ring:
1-2/3 cups water
1 teaspoon salt
1-1/3 cups long-grain rice, uncooked

1 (10-oz.) pkg. frozen peas, uncooked
3 tablespoons butter or margarine

Prepare Rice Ring; set aside in oven. In a medium skillet, melt butter or margarine. Add onion and celery; sauté until tender. With a wire whisk, stir in WHITE SAUCE BUTTER-BALLS and milk, crushing butter-balls. Cook and stir over medium heat until mixture comes to a slow boil. In a small bowl, beat egg yolks. Stir in about 1/2 cup of the white sauce mixture. Stir egg yolk mixture into remaining white sauce mixture. Cook and stir over low heat about 1 minute. Stir in tuna, sliced mushrooms and diced pimiento. Invert molded rice ring onto a large round platter. Shake gently; remove mold. Spoon tuna mixture into Rice Ring. Makes 4 to 6 servings.

Rice Ring:
Very lightly oil a 5-1/2-cup ring mold; set aside. In a large saucepan, bring water to a boil. Stir in salt and rice. Bring water back to a boil. Cover saucepan. Simmer over low heat until water is absorbed and rice is plump and tender. Cook peas in a small amount of lightly salted water until crisp-tender. Drain; discard water. In a large bowl, combine cooked rice, cooked peas and butter or margarine. With a wire whisk, gently stir until evenly distributed. Preheat oven to 250°F (120°C). Press rice mixture into prepared ring mold; cover with foil. Place covered mold in a large shallow baking pan. Pour water 2 inches deep in outer pan. Place mold and pan in preheated oven until ready to serve.

Creamed Vegetables in-a-Ring

Fill the versatile Cheese Puff Ring with any creamed vegetable or meat.

Cheese Puff Ring, see below
10 to 15 small, red-skinned potatoes
1 (10-oz.) pkg. frozen peas or
   1-1/2 cups fresh peas

Cheese Puff Ring:
1 cup water
1/2 cup butter or margarine
1 cup all-purpose flour
1/4 teaspoon salt

8 WHITE SAUCE BUTTER-BALLS,
   page 40
3-1/4 cups milk
1 tablespoon butter

4 eggs
1/3 cup shredded Cheddar cheese
   (1-1/2 oz.)

Prepare Cheese Puff Ring; keep warm. Scrub potatoes with a vegetable brush; cut each in half. In a large pot or Dutch oven, cook cut potatoes in lightly salted water over medium heat until tender, 15 to 20 minutes. In a small saucepan, cook peas in a small amount of lightly salted water over medium heat until crisp-tender, about 8 minutes. In a large saucepan, combine WHITE SAUCE BUTTER-BALLS and 1 cup milk. Use a wire whisk to crush butter-balls. Cook and stir over medium heat until mixture begins to thicken. Do not boil. Gradually stir in remaining milk. Cook and stir until smooth and slightly thickened. Drain potatoes and peas; discard liquid. Stir cooked potatoes and peas into white sauce. Remove Cheese Puff Ring from pie plate; place rounded side up on a platter. Spoon potato mixture into center of ring. Dot surface with butter. Makes 6 to 8 servings.

Cheese Puff Ring:
Preheat oven to 450°F (230°C). Grease a 10-inch pie plate; set aside. In a large saucepan, bring water and butter or margarine to a boil over medium-high heat. Remove from heat. Immediately add flour and salt all at once. Stir vigorously with a wooden spoon until mixture forms a ball and leaves side of pan. Add eggs, one at a time, beating vigorously after each addition. Stir in cheese until melted. Spoon dough in a ring around edge of prepared pie plate, leaving center open. Bake 20 minutes in preheated oven. Reduce heat to 350°F (175°C). Bake 25 to 30 minutes longer, until browned. Turn oven off. Let ring dry in oven with door slightly open, about 15 minutes.

1/Remove boiling mixture from heat. Vigorously stir in all of flour and salt until ball forms.

Navajo Tostadas

The bread in this meatless dish is similar to Navajo fry-bread.

2 cups SOPAIPILLA MIX, page 9
2/3 cup water
Vegetable oil for frying
1 (30-oz.) can refried beans
4 cups shredded Cheddar cheese (1 lb.)

1/2 medium head lettuce, shredded
2 to 3 chopped tomatoes
Salt and pepper to taste
8 ripe olives for garnish

In a medium bowl, combine SOPAIPILLA MIX with water. Stir with a fork until dough forms a ball. Add more water if needed. Turn out onto a lightly floured surface. Knead 8 to 10 times. Divide into 8 pieces. With a rolling pin, roll out each piece to a 6-inch circle; set aside. Cover with a cloth. Pour oil for frying 1 inch deep in a large skillet. Heat to 375°F (190°C). At this temperature a 1-inch cube of bread will turn golden brown in 40 seconds. Use tongs to carefully lower rolled out dough circles into hot oil 1 at a time. Cook until lightly browned on both sides, using tongs to turn once. Drain on paper towels. In a medium skillet or saucepan, heat refried beans over medium heat. Top each fried bread with 1/2 to 3/4 cup hot beans, spreading to cover. Sprinkle each with about 1/2 cup cheese, some of the lettuce and some of the tomatoes. Sprinkle with salt and pepper to taste. Top each with 1 ripe olive. Makes 8 servings.

How to Make Creamed Vegetables in-a-Ring

2/Use 2 spoons to drop mounds of dough around edge of skillet or pie plate.

3/Fill baked ring with creamed vegetables. Garnish with remaining cheese.

Teriyaki Beef & Vegetables

Have the meat and vegetables sliced and the rice cooked before you heat the oil.

1 lb. top sirloin
4 medium carrots
3 medium zucchini
About 1/3 cup vegetable oil
2 tablespoons brown sugar

1-1/2 cups ORIENTAL STIR-FRY MIX,
  page 32
3 cups hot cooked rice
4 green onions, thinly sliced for garnish

On a cutting board, cut meat, carrots and zucchini in thin diagonal slices. Place 3 or 4 paper towels in a medium bowl; set aside. Heat 3 tablespoons oil in a large skillet or wok. Add meat slices; stir constantly over medium heat until meat is no longer red, 3 to 4 minutes. Use a slotted spoon to remove cooked meat to prepared bowl. Cover; keep warm. Add about 2 tablespoons of the remaining oil to skillet or wok. Add carrot slices. Cook and stir 2 to 3 minutes. Add zucchini slices. Cook and stir 2 to 3 minutes longer. Stir in cooked meat, brown sugar and ORIENTAL STIR-FRY MIX. Cook and stir until mixture thickens slightly. Serve over hot cooked rice. Garnish with sliced green onions. Makes 4 to 6 servings.

Easy Beef Stroganoff

Lemon juice adds a slightly piquant flavor.

1 pkg. ALL-PURPOSE GROUND BEEF
  MIX, page 37, thawed
1 (4-oz.) can mushrooms, drained
1-1/3 cups beef broth
2 tablespoons lemon juice
1 cup dairy sour cream

2 tablespoons butter or margarine
1 teaspoon poppy seeds
1 (8-oz.) pkg. medium noodles,
  cooked, drained
Parsley sprigs for garnish

In a large skillet, combine ALL-PURPOSE GROUND BEEF MIX, mushrooms, beef broth and lemon juice. Simmer uncovered over medium heat until heated through, about 5 minutes. Stir in sour cream until just blended and heated through; do not boil. Stir butter or margarine and poppy seeds into hot cooked noodles. Spoon onto a large platter. Spoon meat mixture into a large serving bowl. Garnish with parsley sprigs. Makes 4 to 6 servings.

Spaghetti Royale

Surprise unexpected company with this 30-minute dinner fit for a queen.

4 cups ITALIAN-STYLE MEAT MIX,
  page 38, thawed

1 (12-oz.) pkg. spaghetti, cooked, drained
Grated Romano or Parmesan cheese

In a medium saucepan, simmer ITALIAN-STYLE MEAT MIX over low heat until hot, about 15 to 20 minutes. Pour cooked spaghetti onto a large platter. Spoon sauce over spaghetti. Sprinkle with cheese. Makes 6 to 8 servings.

Sweet & Sour Pork

Serve this tangy sweet and sour sauce over rice, noodles or spaghetti squash.

1 (20-oz.) can pineapple chunks
1 pkg. CUBED PORK MIX,
  page 39, thawed
2 tablespoons white vinegar
1 tablespoon soy sauce
1/3 cup packed brown sugar

1/4 cup ketchup
1 medium green pepper,
  cut in julienne strips
3 cups hot cooked rice

Drain juice from pineapple into a large saucepan. Stir in CUBED PORK MIX, vinegar, soy sauce, brown sugar and ketchup. Stir occasionally over medium heat about 10 minutes. Stir in drained pineapple chunks and green pepper strips. Simmer about 2 minutes until heated through. Serve over hot cooked rice. Makes 4 to 6 servings.

Pork Chow Mein

It takes about thirty minutes to make this Oriental dinner.

1 pkg. CUBED PORK MIX, page 39, thawed
1-1/2 cups water
3 tablespoons soy sauce
4 tablespoons butter or margarine
4 or 5 celery stalks,
  sliced diagonally 1/4-inch thick

1 cup thinly sliced fresh mushrooms
1 (8-oz.) can water chestnuts,
  drained, thinly sliced
2 cups fresh bean sprouts
4 green onions, thinly sliced
1 (9-1/2-oz.) can chow mein noodles

In a large saucepan, combine CUBED PORK MIX, water and soy sauce. Simmer over low heat about 5 minutes. In a medium skillet, melt butter or margarine. Add celery; sauté until crisp-tender, about 10 minutes. Add fresh mushrooms and water chestnuts. Sauté 2 minutes, stirring occasionally. Stir into pork mixture. Stir occasionally over medium heat 5 minutes. Gently stir in bean sprouts and green onion slices. Simmer 1 minute longer. Serve over chow mein noodles. Makes about 6 servings.

Oriental-Style Hamburger Skillet

If you prefer a crunchier texture, serve this mixture over Chinese-style noodles.

1 pkg. ALL-PURPOSE GROUND BEEF
  MIX, page 37, thawed
3-1/2 cups water

2-1/4 cups instant rice
1/4 cup soy sauce
Salt to taste

In a large skillet, combine ALL-PURPOSE GROUND BEEF MIX, water, rice and soy sauce. Stirring occasionally, cook over medium heat until water is absorbed and rice is tender, about 10 minutes. Stir in salt to taste. Makes 4 to 6 servings.

Quick Chow Mein

For an even quicker meal, use canned chow mein vegetables.

1 (4-oz.) can mushroom pieces, drained
1 teaspoon ground ginger
2 tablespoons soy sauce
2 cups beef broth
1 pkg. CUBED PORK MIX, page 39, or
   ALL-PURPOSE GROUND BEEF
   MIX, page 37, thawed
2 cups shredded Chinese cabbage
2 cups chopped celery
1/2 lb. fresh bean sprouts

1 (8-oz.) can water chestnuts,
   drained, sliced
2 tablespoons cornstarch
1/4 cup cold water
3 cups hot cooked rice
3 tablespoons snipped fresh parsley
   for garnish
2 tablespoons sliced blanched almonds
   for garnish

In a large skillet or wok, combine mushrooms, ginger, soy sauce and beef broth. Cover and simmer over medium heat 5 minutes. Add CUBED PORK MIX or ALL-PURPOSE GROUND BEEF MIX, cabbage, celery, bean sprouts and water chestnuts. Simmer until vegetables are hot, about 5 minutes. Stir cornstarch into cold water to dissolve. Stir into meat mixture. Continue stirring until mixture boils. Cover; simmer over low heat 5 minutes longer. Serve over hot cooked rice. Garnish with snipped parsley and sliced almonds. Makes 6 to 8 servings.

How to Make Quick Chow Mein

1/Add mix and vegetables to broth mixture. Simmer until vegetables are crisp-tender.

2/Serve over hot rice. Garnish with snipped parsley and sliced almonds.

Stroganoff Beef Crepes

Store fresh mushrooms in the refrigerator in a brown paper bag to keep them fresh.

Basic Crepes, see below
4 tablespoons butter or margarine
1/2 lb. fresh mushrooms, washed, sliced
1/2 cup beef broth
1 tablespoon ketchup

1 tablespoon Worcestershire sauce
1 pkg. CUBED BEEF MIX,
  page 37, thawed
1 cup dairy sour cream
Parsley for garnish

Basic Crepes:
1-1/4 cups all-purpose flour
Pinch salt
3 eggs, beaten

1-1/2 cups milk
2 tablespoons butter or margarine, melted

Prepare crepes. In a large skillet, melt butter or margarine. Add mushrooms. Sauté over low heat until tender but not browned; set aside. In a small saucepan, bring broth to a boil. Stir broth into sautéed mushrooms. Stir in ketchup, Worcestershire sauce and CUBED BEEF MIX. Continue cooking until heated through. Gently stir in sour cream; do not boil. Arrange 12 crepes in a single layer on a flat surface. Spoon about 1/4 cup beef mixture into center of each crepe. Roll up jelly-roll fashion. Place filled crepes on a platter. Wrap remaining crepes in heavy-duty foil and freeze. Spoon remaining sauce over rolled crepes. Garnish with parsley. Makes about 6 servings.

Basic Crepes:

In a blender, combine all ingredients. Process on high speed about 30 seconds. Use a rubber spatula to scrape down sides, if necessary. Cover; let stand 1 hour. Bake on a crepe maker or in a crepe pan following manufacturers directions. Makes 20 crepes.

Bunwiches

Slice a loaf of french bread in half lengthwise, then spread the cut sides with this mixture.

1 pkg. ALL-PURPOSE GROUND BEEF
  MIX, page 37, thawed
1 (8-oz.) can tomato sauce
3 hard-cooked eggs, chopped
1 (2-oz.) jar pimiento-stuffed
  green olives, sliced

2 cups shredded Cheddar cheese (8 oz.)
6 French rolls or onion rolls, split,
  toasted, buttered

In a medium saucepan, gently combine ALL-PURPOSE GROUND BEEF MIX, tomato sauce, chopped eggs and sliced olives. Stir occasionally over medium heat about 10 minutes. Stir in cheese until it begins to melt. Spoon evenly onto bottom portions of rolls. Cover with tops of rolls. Serve immediately. Makes 6 servings.

Variation

In a medium saucepan, combine 1 pkg. ALL-PURPOSE GROUND BEEF MIX, 3 tablespoons ketchup and 3/4 cup Cheddar cheese cubes. Stir occasionally over medium heat until cheese begins to melt, about 10 minutes. Spoon onto bottom portions of 6 hamburger buns. Cover with tops of buns. Makes 6 servings.

English Poached Eggs & Ham

Poach eggs in simmering water or in lightly buttered egg poacher cups.

3 English muffins
1 pkg. FREEZER CHEESE SAUCE MIX,
   page 36, thawed
6 eggs

6 slices ham
6 cherry tomatoes for garnish
6 parsley sprigs for garnish

Cut muffins in half. In broiler or toaster, lightly toast muffin halves. Place each half on a separate plate. In a small saucepan, warm FREEZER CHEESE SAUCE MIX over low heat. Pour water 1-1/2 inches deep in a medium skillet. Bring to a simmer over medium-high heat; do not boil. Break 1 egg into a small bowl or custard cup. Carefully pour egg into simmering water. Cook until egg white is set but tender and egg yolk is slightly set, 3 to 5 minutes. If desired, poach several eggs at once, not letting eggs touch one another. Lift poached eggs from water with a slotted spoon or spatula. Drain on paper towels. Spoon 2 tablespoons of the warmed FREEZER CHEESE SAUCE MIX over each muffin half. Top each with 1 slice ham and 1 poached egg. Spoon remaining sauce evenly over eggs. Garnish each serving with 1 cherry tomato and 1 parsley sprig. Makes 6 servings.

Puffy Omelet

The perfect brunch idea when everyone gets a late start.

1 tablespoon butter or margarine
1 cup thinly sliced fresh mushrooms
1/2 cup chopped green pepper
6 eggs, separated, room temperature
1/8 teaspoon cream of tartar
1/2 teaspoon salt
Pinch pepper

1/3 cup milk
1 tablespoon butter or margarine
1 tablespoon vegetable oil
1 pkg. FREEZER CHEESE SAUCE MIX,
   page 36, thawed
1/2 cup chopped tomatoes

Preheat oven to 350°F (175°C). In a small skillet, melt 1 tablespoon butter or margarine. Add mushrooms and green pepper. Sauté until crisp-tender. Drain; set aside. In a large bowl, beat egg whites with cream of tartar until stiff peaks form. In a small bowl, beat egg yolks until thick and pale. Gradually beat in salt, pepper and milk until blended. Using a wire whisk, gently fold egg yolk mixture into beaten egg whites. In a large skillet or omelet pan with an oven-proof handle, heat 1 tablespoon butter or margarine and oil until hot, but not browned. Tilt pan to coat sides. Spread egg mixture evenly in pan. Without stirring, cook over low heat until lightly browned on bottom, about 8 minutes. Place skillet or omelet pan in preheated oven. Bake 8 to 10 minutes until top feels somewhat firm when pressed with your fingers. In a small saucepan, heat FREEZER CHEESE SAUCE MIX over low heat, stirring occasionally. Invert omelet onto a large platter. Spoon sauce over omelet. Sprinkle top evenly with tomatoes and sautéed mushrooms and green peppers. Cut in wedges to serve. Makes 4 to 6 servings.

Smothered Hamburger Patties

Searing *means to cook for a short time at a high temperature to form a brown crust.*

2 lbs. lean ground beef
2 tablespoons vegetable shortening
1/3 cup all-purpose flour
1-1/4 cups Creamed Mushroom Sauce,
   page 62, or 1 (10-1/2-oz.)
   can condensed cream of mushroom soup

1-1/3 cups water
1/2 cup BEEF GRAVY MIX, page 31

Preheat oven to 350°F (175°C). Form ground beef into 8 to 10 patties. In a large skillet, melt shortening. Dip each patty in flour, coating both sides. Sear in hot shortening, turning once. Arrange seared patties in a 13" x 9" baking dish. In a medium saucepan, combine sauce or soup, water and BEEF GRAVY MIX. Stir with a wire whisk over medium heat until slightly thickened. Pour evenly over meat. Cover and bake 1 hour in preheated oven. Makes 6 to 8 servings.

Cathy's Meatball Sandwiches

This knife and fork sandwich is a big hit with teenagers.

4 cups ITALIAN-STYLE MEAT MIX,
   page 38, thawed
1 tablespoon butter or margarine

1 cup fresh mushrooms, thinly sliced
6 to 8 French rolls or onion rolls, split
1/4 cup grated Romano cheese

In a medium saucepan, bring ITALIAN-STYLE MEAT MIX to a boil, about 10 minutes. In a small skillet, melt butter or margarine. Add mushrooms; sauté until tender, about 2 minutes. Spoon meat mixture evenly on bottom portions of rolls. Spoon sautéed mushrooms evenly over meat mixture. Sprinkle evenly with cheese. Cover with tops of rolls. Makes 6 to 8 servings.

Shrimp & Vegetable Stir-Fry

For a less expensive dish, substitute frozen cooked shrimp for the fresh shrimp.

About 1-1/4 lbs. broccoli
4 tablespoons vegetable oil
1 medium onion, thinly sliced
3/4 lb. fresh mushrooms, thinly sliced
2 tablespoons vegetable oil

3/4 lb. fresh shrimp, shelled, deveined
1-1/2 cups ORIENTAL STIR-FRY MIX,
   page 32, thawed
2 cups fresh bean sprouts
3 cups hot cooked rice

Cut broccoli stems into 1/4-inch pieces. Cut flowerets into 3/4-inch pieces; set aside. In a large skillet or wok, heat 4 tablespoons oil over medium heat. Add cut broccoli stems, sliced onion and sliced mushrooms. Cook and stir until stems are crisp-tender, 5 to 7 minutes. Add 2 tablespoons oil. When oil is hot, add shrimp and broccoli flowerets. Cook and stir 5 to 7 minutes longer. Spoon ORIENTAL STIR-FRY MIX over vegetables. Stir gently until mixture thickens slightly. Gently stir in bean sprouts; cook 1 minute longer. To serve, spoon hot mixture over cooked rice. Makes 4 to 6 servings.

Meat, Fish & Poultry

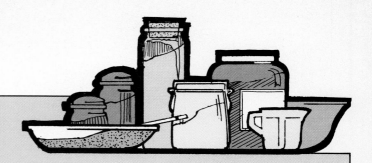

The greater part of most food budgets is spent for meat, so you want to get the most meat for your food dollar. Price per pound is not always the best clue to value. Even so, less-tender meat usually costs less than tender cuts. For this reason, we recommend chuck roast, flank steak, arm roast, brisket and lean chuck beef cubes.

Flank steak is an oval, boneless, flat steak with coarse muscle fibers running lengthwise through the meat. In Marinated Flank Steak, the meat is marinated overnight before being broiled or grilled. Marinades are usually made from an acid such as vinegar, wine or citrus juice combined with oil and a variety of spices. The acid tenderizes the meat while the spices flavor it. Once you've used it, MARINADE BLEND MIX, page 31, will become your answer to tenderizing all less-tender cuts of meat.

There was a time when poultry cost more than meat or fish. A French king and an American president promised their people *"a chicken in every pot!"* or in other words, prosperity. With the development of meatier, broad-chested chickens and improved feeding and marketing practices, the price of chicken fell and those promises were kept. Since that time, the lofty chicken has moved out of the *pot* and into the *skillet or oven.* Its flavor, shape and texture can be altered by boning, pounding, wrapping, dipping and coating. Easy recipes in this section use all of these alterations. If you prefer a crisp coating, try Crunchy-Crust Chicken. It is dipped in an egg mixture and CRISP COATING MIX, page 19, then baked.

Stuffing is often served as a side dish with poultry or pork. When baked with these meats, juices soak into the dressing giving it an unforgetable flavor. Stuffing also needs other flavorings. To prevent a last-minute search for the right spice blend, use STUFFING SEASONING MIX, page 20, with bread cubes, or Saucepan Stuffing, page 20, as in Stuffed Pork Chops.

Crunchy Fish Bake

To keep the juices in, cover the fish fillets completely with egg mixture and mix.

2-1/2 tablespoons butter or margarine	**2 eggs**
2-1/2 tablespoons vegetable oil	**1 tablespoon milk**
1-1/2 cups CRISP COATING MIX, page 19	**1-1/2 lbs. boneless red snapper, sole, halibut or turbot fillets**

Preheat oven to 500°F (260°C). Combine butter or margarine and oil on a large baking sheet with raised sides. Place in preheating oven until hot but not browned. Pour CRISP COATING MIX into a large plastic food storage bag; set aside. In a shallow bowl, beat eggs and milk until blended. Rinse fish; pat dry with paper towels. Dip each fish fillet in egg mixture; drain briefly. Place 1 fillet at a time in plastic bag, shaking until evenly coated. Arrange on baking sheet, turning to coat with oil mixture. Bake 7 to 10 minutes in preheated oven until fish flakes when tested with a fork, turning once. Makes 4 to 6 servings.

Apricot Chicken

Use pineapple tidbits and orange marmalade in place of apricot halves and apricot jam.

2 (3-lb.) frying chickens, cut up
1 pkg. FRENCH-ITALIAN SALAD
   DRESSING MIX, page 17
1/4 cup red wine vinegar
1/2 cup ketchup

1 (16-oz.) can apricot halves, drained
1 cup apricot jam
1 pkg. ONION SEASONING MIX,
   page 19
Parsley sprigs for garnish

Preheat oven to 350°F (175°C). Rinse chickens. Pat dry with paper towels; set aside. In a medium bowl, combine FRENCH-ITALIAN SALAD DRESSING MIX, vinegar, ketchup, apricot halves, apricot jam and ONION SEASONING MIX. Place chicken pieces on 2 ungreased large baking sheets with raised sides. Pour sauce evenly over chicken pieces. Bake uncovered 1-1/4 hours in preheated oven until chicken is lightly browned. Arrange baked chicken on a large platter. Spoon drippings over chicken pieces. Garnish with parsley sprigs. Makes 8 servings.

Variation

Substitute 1 (8-ounce) bottle Russian salad dressing for FRENCH-ITALIAN SALAD DRESSING MIX, vinegar and ketchup.

Wrapped Chicken Breasts

These bacon-wrapped breasts are tender and flavorful.

3 whole chicken breasts, skinned
1 (2-oz.) pkg. thinly sliced smoked beef
6 bacon slices
2 cups milk
4 WHITE SAUCE BUTTER-BALLS,
   page 40

1-1/2 teaspoons instant chicken
   bouillon granules
1 teaspoon dried parsley leaves
1 (4-oz.) can mushrooms, drained
1 cup dairy sour cream
Paprika

Lightly grease a 13" x 9" baking dish. Cut chicken breasts in half lenthwise. Remove bone, if desired; set aside. Arrange sliced beef over bottom of baking dish. Wrap each chicken breast in 1 slice bacon with ends under breasts. Arrange over sliced beef. In a medium saucepan, combine milk, WHITE SAUCE BUTTER-BALLS and bouillon granules. Use a wire whisk to crush butter-balls. Stir constantly over medium heat until slightly thickened and smooth. Remove from heat. Preheat oven to 300°F (150°C). Stir parsley, mushrooms and sour cream into white sauce. Pour over chicken breasts. Sprinkle with paprika. Bake uncovered 1-1/2 hours in preheated oven until golden brown and tender. Makes 6 servings.

Skin is easily pulled from chicken pieces or a whole chicken. To remove bone from chicken, carefully pull bone and chicken apart, or use a small sharp knife to cut the meat free from the bone.

Apricot Chicken

Chicken Breasts en Croûte

Have your butcher skin and bone the chicken breasts for you.

3 whole chicken breasts, skinned, boned
2 tablespoons vegetable oil
1 tablespoon freshly snipped parsley leaves
Salt and pepper to taste

1 (3-oz.) pkg. cream cheese with chives
1 (6-pack) box frozen patty shells,
 slightly thawed
Chicken Gravy, page 28

Cut chicken breasts in half lengthwise; set aside. Preheat oven to 400°F (205°C). Heat oil in a large skillet. Add breast halves. Sear over high heat 3 to 4 minutes, turning once. Stir in snipped parsley and salt and pepper to taste. Remove seared chicken from pan; cool slightly. Cut cream cheese into 6 equal pieces. Insert 1 piece into underside indentation of each half chicken breast. Between 2 sheets of waxed paper, roll out each patty shell to an 8-inch circle. Wrap each breast in 1 pastry circle. Pinch edges together to seal. Place wrapped breasts, seam-side down, on an ungreased baking sheet. Bake 35 to 40 minutes in preheated oven until golden brown. Place baked chicken on a platter. Cover evenly with Chicken Gravy. Makes 6 servings.

Chicken in Mushroom Sauce

Serve this company dish with a mixture of cooked white and wild rice.

1/4 cup butter or margarine
1 (3-lb.) chicken, cut up
1/2 cup CHICKEN GRAVY MIX, page 28
2 cups dairy sour cream
1 cup milk

1/2 lb. fresh mushrooms, sliced
1 tablespoon freshly snipped parsley
1 tablespoon poppy seeds
1 tablespoon lemon juice
Grated peel of 1/2 lemon (3/4 teaspoon)

Preheat oven to 325°F (165°C). In a large skillet, melt butter or margarine. Add chicken pieces. Cook over medium heat until browned. Remove chicken from skillet; arrange in a large casserole dish. Stir CHICKEN GRAVY MIX into pan drippings. Blend in sour cream and milk. Stirring constantly, simmer 3 to 5 minutes. Do not boil. Pour sauce evenly over chicken. Sprinkle with mushrooms, parsley and poppy seeds. Cover and bake 30 to 45 minutes until tender. Sprinkle lemon juice and lemon peel over casserole. Serve immediately. Makes 6 servings.

Crunchy-Crust Chicken

To get an extra-crisp surface, double-dip the chicken in the egg and mix.

1-1/2 cups CRISP COATING MIX,
 page 19
2 eggs

1 tablespoon milk
1 (2-1/2-lb.) broiler-fryer chicken,
 cut up

Preheat oven to 400°F (205°C). Lightly grease a baking sheet; set aside. Pour CRISP COATING MIX into a large plastic food storage bag; set aside. In a shallow bowl, beat eggs and milk until blended. Rinse chicken; pat dry with paper towels. Dip each piece of chicken in egg mixture; drain briefly. Place 2 to 3 pieces at a time in plastic bag, shaking until evenly coated. Remove chicken from bag; arrange on prepared baking sheet. Cover with foil. Bake 40 minutes. Remove foil and bake 10 to 20 minutes longer until golden brown and crisp. Makes 4 to 6 servings.

Chicken & Ham Foldovers

Make these the night before, then refrigerate them until you're ready to begin baking.

3 whole chicken breasts, skinned, boned
3/4 cup CRISP COATING MIX, page 19,
  or 3/4 cup crushed corn flakes
6 thin slices ham
6 thin slices Swiss cheese

3 tablespoons butter or margarine, melted
1 cup CHICKEN GRAVY MIX, page 28
2 cups water
10 cherry tomatoes for garnish
4 parsley sprigs for garnish

Lightly butter a 13" x 9" baking dish; set aside. Cut chicken breasts in half lengthwise. Place each half between 2 layers of waxed paper or plastic wrap. Using a meat mallet or another heavy flat object, pound to a 7" x 4" rectangle. Preheat oven to 350°F (175°C). Pour CRISP COATING MIX or cornflakes into a pie plate; set aside. Cut ham slices and cheese slices in half. On 1 side of each flattened chicken breast, layer 1 piece of ham and 1 piece of cheese. Repeat layers. Fold chicken breast over layered ham and cheese pieces. Brush melted butter or margarine evenly over folded chicken breasts. Press each folded breast into CRISP COATING MIX or cornflakes. Arrange in prepared baking dish. Bake 30 minutes in preheated oven. In a small saucepan, combine CHICKEN GRAVY MIX and water. Cook and stir over medium heat until smooth and slightly thickened. Pour over partially cooked chicken breasts. Cover and bake about 30 minutes longer until tender. To serve, arrange baked chicken breasts on a platter. Garnish with cherry tomatoes and parsley sprigs. Makes 6 servings.

How to Make Chicken & Ham Foldovers

1/Use rolling pin or meat mallet to pound chicken breasts between plastic wrap until thin.

2/On flattened breast, layer ham and cheese. Fold in half. Coat with butter or margarine and CRISP COATING MIX.

Company Beef Brisket

Begin baking the brisket in the morning so it will be ready for your evening meal.

1 (5-lb.) beef brisket
1 pkg. ONION SEASONING MIX,
  page 19
2 tablespoons water
1 teaspoon salt

1/4 teaspoon pepper
3 tablespoons butter or margarine
10 small boiling onions, peeled
1/4 lb. small fresh mushrooms

Preheat oven to 350°F (175°C). Cut two 18" x 12" pieces of heavy-duty foil. Place 1 piece of foil on a large baking sheet with raised sides. Place brisket in center of foil. Sprinkle evenly with ONION SEASONING MIX, water, salt and pepper. Cut 1 tablespoon butter or margarine in pieces; dot evenly over meat. Bring 2 short ends of foil together over meat. Fold tight against meat; fold sides to make a tight seal. Repeat with second piece of foil, making a double covering of foil. Bake 1 hour in preheated oven. Reduce heat to 250°F (120°C). Bake 9 hours longer. In a medium saucepan, melt remaining 2 tablespoons butter or margarine. Add boiling onions. Sauté until tender when pierced with a fork. Add mushrooms; sauté 3 or 4 minutes longer. Unwrap meat. Pour drippings into onion mixture, stirring to combine. Slice meat, arranging slices on a platter. To serve, pour onion mixture over sliced brisket. Makes 18 to 20 servings.

Variation

To cook a 3- or 4-pound brisket, bake 30 minutes in preheated oven at 350°F (175°C), then 5 or 6 hours longer at 250°F (120°C).

Onion Pot Roast

Thicken the drippings with a cornstarch-water mixture to make a tasty gravy.

1/2 teaspoon salt
Pinch pepper
3 to 4 lbs. beef arm roast or
  7 blade pot roast
3 tablespoons all-purpose flour or
  whole-wheat flour
3 tablespoons vegetable shortening

1 pkg. ONION SEASONING MIX,
  page 19
1 cup water
4 medium carrots, peeled, quartered
3 celery stalks, cut in sticks
3 medium potatoes, cut in half
1 bay leaf

Preheat oven to 325°F (165°C). Sprinkle salt and pepper over roast. Dredge in flour, turning to coat all sides. In a Dutch oven, melt shortening over medium heat. Add roast, turning to brown all sides. In a small bowl, combine ONION SEASONING MIX and water. Pour over roast. Add carrots, celery, potatoes and bay leaf; cover. Bake 3 hours until meat is tender. On a platter, arrange cooked vegetables around roast. Serve immediately. Makes 6 to 8 servings.

Variation

Foil-Wrapped Chuck Steak: Substitute 3 pounds chuck steak about 1 inch thick for roast. Omit flour and shortening. Reduce water to 1/2 cup. Place steak on an 18" x 12" rectangle of heavy-duty foil in a large baking pan. Sprinkle meat with ONION SEASONING MIX, salt and pepper. Carefully pour water over steak. Arrange carrots, celery and potatoes over steak. Dot with 2 tablespoons butter or margarine. Fold foil tightly against meat and vegetables. Bake 2 to 2-1/2 hours at 450°F (230°C). Serve as directed above. Makes 6 servings.

No-Fuss Swiss Steak Cubes

Put everything but the noodles in a Dutch oven and let it simmer 4 hours.

2 lbs. lean beef, cut in 1-1/2-inch cubes
3 tablespoons all-purpose flour
1 (4-oz.) can diced or
   chopped green chilies
1 pkg. ONION SEASONING MIX,
   page 19

1/2 lb. fresh mushrooms or
   1 (8-oz.) can mushrooms, drained
1 (28-oz.) can tomatoes, crushed
2 cups water
3 cups hot cooked noodles, buttered

Dredge beef cubes in flour; place in Dutch oven. Add green chilies, ONION SEASONING MIX, mushrooms, tomatoes and water. Stir to blend. Cover; place in cold oven. Turn oven to 300°F (150°C). Bake 3 to 4 hours until tender. After 2 hours, add more water if needed to keep mixture moist. Serve over hot buttered noodles. Makes 6 to 8 servings.

Easy-Bake Pork Chops

As you trim the pork chops, leave on a little fat to prevent them from becoming dry.

2-1/2 tablespoons butter or margarine
2-1/2 tablespoons vegetable oil
1-1/2 cups CRISP COATING MIX,
   page 19

2 eggs
1 tablespoon milk
6 pork chops, shoulder cut, 3/4 inch thick

Preheat oven to 400°F (205°C). Combine butter or margarine and oil on large baking sheet with raised edges. Place in preheating oven until hot but not browned. Pour CRISP COATING MIX into a large plastic food storage bag; set aside. In a shallow bowl, beat eggs and milk until blended. Rinse pork chops; pat dry with paper towels. Dip each pork chop in egg mixture; drain briefly. Place 1 pork chop at a time in plastic bag, shaking until evenly coated. Arrange on baking sheet, turning to coat with oil mixture. Bake 30 minutes in preheated oven until golden brown and crispy, turning once. Makes 4 to 6 servings.

Marinated Flank Steak

Less tender cuts of meat such as flank steak are tenderized in the marinade.

1-1/2 lbs. flank steak
1 cup MARINADE BLEND MIX,
   page 31

5 green onions, finely chopped
2 tablespoons honey
1/4 cup soy sauce

Place steak in a 13" x 9" baking dish. In a small bowl, combine MARINADE BLEND MIX, onions, honey, and soy sauce. Pour over steak. Cover and refrigerate overnight. Preheat broiler or grill. Broil or grill about 7 minutes on each side for medium. Makes 4 to 6 servings.

Variation

Marinated Chuck Roast: In a 13" x 9" baking dish, pour 1-1/2 cups MARINADE BLEND MIX over a 3-pound chuck roast, 1-1/2 inches thick. Cover and refrigerate at least 10 hours, turning once. Broil or grill about 10 minutes on each side for medium. Makes 6 to 8 servings.

Football Hero

This hamburger pattie served in Football Hero Bun, page 104, will feed six people.

1 pkg. ONION SEASONING MIX, page 19
3/4 cup finely chopped celery
1-3/4 lbs. lean ground beef
1/4 cup dry breadcrumbs
1 egg, slightly beaten
4 slices cheese
Football Hero Bun, page 104

4 large tomato slices
4 large onion slices
2 tablespoons chili sauce
1/4 cup pickle slices, drained
4 large lettuce leaves
Parsley for garnish

In a large bowl, combine ONION SEASONING MIX, celery, ground beef, breadcrumbs and egg. Shape into a 10-inch pattie. In a large skillet, fry pattie until browned on both sides and no longer pink. Drain drippings from skillet. Arrange cheese slices evenly over pattie. Cover skillet. Cook until cheese melts, about 1 minute. Cut Football Hero Bun in half horizontally. Place bottom half on a large platter. Place cooked pattie on bottom half of cut bun. On top of meat, arrange tomato slices, onion slices, chili sauce, pickle slices and lettuce. Place top of bun on pattie. Garnish with parsley. To serve, cut in wedges. Makes 6 servings.

Tasty Beef Roll-Ups

Serve with Old-Fashioned Vegetable Platter, page 70.

1 cup dry breadcrumbs
1/4 cup shredded Cheddar cheese (1 oz.)
1/4 cup butter or margarine, melted
2 tablespoons chopped green onion

6 thin cubed steaks
3 tablespoons vegetable oil
1 cup BEEF GRAVY MIX, page 31
2 cups cold water

In a medium bowl, combine breadcrumbs, cheese, melted butter or margarine and green onions. Arrange steaks on a flat surface. Spread evenly with breadcrumb mixture. Roll up jelly-roll fashion. Fasten with a wooden pick or a skewer. Heat oil in a medium skillet. Add rolled steaks. Cook over medium heat until browned. In a small saucepan, blend BEEF GRAVY MIX and water. Stir over medium heat with a wire whisk until smooth and slightly thickened. Pour gravy over steaks. Cover and simmer 25 to 30 minutes until steaks are tender. Makes 6 servings.

Stuffed Pork Chops

Your butcher will cut pockets in the pork chops if you ask him.

4 pork chops, 1 to 1-1/2 inches thick   **1/2 cup BEEF GRAVY MIX, page 31**
Saucepan Stuffing, page 20

Lightly butter a 9-inch square baking dish; set aside. Cut pockets in sides of pork chops, 3 inches wide and 2-1/2 inches deep. Preheat oven to 350°F (175°C). Spoon 3 to 4 tablespoons stuffing into each pocket. Turn remaining stuffing into bottom of prepared baking dish. Pat BEEF GRAVY MIX evenly over all sides of stuffed pork chops. Arrange coated chops over stuffing. Cover with foil. Bake about 1-1/2 hours in preheated oven until well-browned. Serve in baking dish or place chops on a platter and stuffing in a serving bowl. Makes 4 servings.

How to Make Stuffed Pork Chops

1/Using a sharp knife, cut large pockets in side of each pork chop.

2/Stuff pockets. Pat BEEF GRAVY MIX over stuffed chops. Place on stuffing in baking pan.

Baking

WHOLE-WHEAT HOT ROLL MIX, page 33, gives tender and delicious breads and rolls. Recipes from HOT ROLL MIX in our first *Make-a-Mix Cookery* were tested and worked well.

Some people shy away from making bread, thinking it is too difficult. If you use the right ingredients and methods, you cannot fail. Patience is the most important "ingredient" in bread making. If you are a novice baker, it may take you four hours from start to finish to make Giant Braided Loaf, but it is well worth the effort.

Have your mix at room temperature before you begin. Combine ingredients thoroughly, adding enough flour to make a soft but not sticky dough. Turn it out on a lightly floured surface. Knead the dough about 10 minutes. Kneading stretches the gluten in the flour, making it strong but pliable. To knead, fold the dough opposite you up and on top of the dough closest to you. Press the layers together with the heels of your hands. Turn the dough 1/4 turn. Repeat folding, pressing and turning. Well-kneaded dough is smooth with small air bubbles under the surface.

Let the dough rise in a clean, greased bowl until doubled in bulk. *Proof* it or test its readiness by pressing two fingers about 2-1/2 inches deep in the center of the dough. If the dough springs back most of the way, let it rise longer. If most of the indentation remains, your dough is ready to shape into rolls, pan loaves or braids. After shaping, let it rise until almost doubled.

You will appreciate the ease of making quick breads with SWEET QUICK BREAD MIX, page 11, and SOPAIPILLA MIX, page 9. Aebleskivers are a quick bread and a change from pancakes for breakfast. An aebleskiver pan looks like a heavy muffin tin with shallow cups. Season it well before using by pouring unsalted oil in the cups and heating it in a 250°F (120°C) oven 2 hours. Reseason the pan as needed.

Hamburger Buns

Make hot dog buns by shaping the dough into logs.

3 pkgs. active dry yeast (3 tablespoons)
1-1/2 cups lukewarm water (110°F, 45°C)
2 eggs, beaten
1/2 cup vegetable oil

5 to 6 cups WHOLE-WHEAT
  HOT ROLL MIX, page 33
2 tablespoons butter or margarine, melted

In a large bowl, stir yeast into lukewarm water until softened. Stir in eggs and oil. Beat in 5 cups of the WHOLE-WHEAT HOT ROLL MIX until blended. Let rest 2 minutes. Add enough of the remaining mix to make a soft dough. Knead until smooth, 7 to 10 minutes. Clean and grease bowl. Place dough in bowl, turning to grease all sides. Cover with a damp towel. Let rise in a warm place, free from drafts, until doubled in bulk. Grease 2 baking sheets; set aside. Punch down dough. Let rest 10 minutes. Use a rolling pin to roll out dough 1/2 inch thick. Cut buns with a large can or bun cutter, or divide dough into 12 equal pieces, shaping each into a 4-inch circle, 1/2 inch thick. Let rise 10 to 15 minutes. Preheat oven to 425°F (220°C). Bake 10 minutes until golden brown. Remove from baking sheets; cool on a rack. To keep the buns soft, brush with butter or margarine then cover with a dry cloth. Makes twelve 5-inch buns.

Sopaipillas   Photo on page 105.

If the sopaipillas don't rise to the top immediately, the oil is not hot enough.

2 cups SOPAIPILLA MIX, page 9   **Oil for frying**
About 2/3 cup water   **Powdered sugar for garnish**

In a medium bowl, combine SOPAIPILLA MIX and 2/3 cup water. Mix with a fork until dough clings together. Add more water, if needed. Turn out dough on a lightly floured surface. Knead 8 to 10 times. Cover; let rest 20 minutes. Pour oil for frying 2 to 3 inches deep in a medium skillet. Heat to 375°F (190°C). At this temperature, a 1-inch cube of bread will turn golden brown in 40 seconds. With a pizza cutter or knife, cut dough into 3-inch squares. Use tongs to carefully lower squares into hot oil. When puffed, turn to brown other side. Drain on paper towels. Sprinkle with powdered sugar. Serve hot. Makes about 20 sopaipillas.

Pocket Bread

Your own imagination is the only limitation for using this bread.

1 pkg. active dry yeast (1 tablespoon)   **Cornmeal or flour**
1 cup lukewarm water (110°F, 45°C)   **Mayonnaise, cream cheese, butter or**
2 tablespoons vegetable oil   **margarine**
2 to 2-1/2 cups WHOLE-WHEAT   **Fillings for Pocket Breads, see below**
HOT ROLL MIX, page 33

In a medium bowl, stir yeast into lukewarm water until softened. Beat in oil and 2 cups WHOLE-WHEAT HOT ROLL MIX. Stir in enough of the remaining mix to make a soft dough. Turn out on a lightly floured surface. Knead until smooth, 7 to 10 minutes. Clean and grease bowl. Place dough in bowl, turning to grease all sides. Cover with a damp towel. Let rise in a warm place, free from drafts, until doubled in bulk, 1 to 1-1/2 hours. Punch down dough. Divide into 8 equal pieces. Shape each piece into a ball. Cover with a towel and let rest 30 minutes. Sprinkle 4 large baking sheets with cornmeal or flour; set aside. On a lightly floured surface, roll out each ball to an 8-inch circle, not more than 1/8 inch thick. Arrange several inches apart on prepared baking sheets. Cover with towels. Let rise 30 minutes. Preheat oven to 500°F (260°C). Bake bread on bottom rack of oven 4 to 5 minutes, then on middle rack 2 to 3 minutes or until puffed and delicately browned. Remove from baking sheets. Wrap warm bread in foil or place in a plastic food bag to keep surface soft. Serve warm or at room temperature. Will keep in refrigerator several days. To serve, spread insides of cut pocket bread with mayonnaise, cream cheese or butter or margarine. Fill with 1 of the filling combinations below. Makes 8 pocket breads.

Fillings for Pocket Breads:
Fresh Vegetable Filling: Combine 2 chopped avocados, 2 cups alfalfa sprouts, 1 cup sliced fresh mushrooms and 2 thinly sliced tomatoes. Spoon evenly into 8 pocket breads.
Taco Filling: Cook 1 pound ground beef. Stir in 1 (1-1/4-ounce) package taco seasoning. Layer evenly in 8 pocket breads, cooked taco-seasoned meat, 2 cups shredded lettuce, 1-1/2 cups shredded Monterey Jack cheese, 2 chopped tomatoes and 1/2 cup dairy sour cream.
Bean Filling: Layer evenly in 8 pocket breads, 2 cups hot refried beans, 1-1/2 cup shredded Cheddar cheese and 2 cups shredded lettuce.
Salad Filling: Combine 2 cups chopped chicken, chopped ham or tuna, 2 chopped hard-cooked eggs, 1/2 cup finely diced celery, 2 tablespoons lemon juice, 1/2 to 3/4 cup mayonnaise and salt and pepper to taste. Spoon evenly into 8 pocket breads.

Whole-Wheat Cinnamon Rolls

Simple, self-frosting and delicious!

1 pkg. active dry yeast (1 tablespoon)
1-1/2 cups lukewarm water (110°F, 45°C)
2 eggs, beaten
1/2 cup butter or margarine, melted, or
  1/2 cup vegetable oil

5 to 6 cups WHOLE-WHEAT
  HOT ROLL MIX, page 33
Cinnamon Butter, see below
Caramel Topping, see below

Cinnamon Butter:
5 tablespoons butter or margarine
1 teaspoon ground cinnamon
1/2 cup packed brown sugar

3/4 cup raisins
1/2 cup chopped nuts

Caramel Topping:
1 cup whipping cream
1/2 cup packed brown sugar

1/2 cup chopped nuts

In a large bowl, stir yeast into lukewarm water until softened. Stir in eggs and butter or margarine or oil. Beat in 5 cups WHOLE-WHEAT HOT ROLL MIX. Let rest 2 minutes. Add enough of the remaining mix to make a soft dough. Turn out onto a lightly floured surface. Knead until smooth, 7 to 10 minutes. Clean and grease bowl. Place dough in bowl, turning to grease all sides. Cover with a damp towel. Let rise in a warm place, free from drafts, until doubled in bulk. Prepare Cinnamon Butter and Caramel Topping; set aside. Punch down dough. Let rest 10 minutes. On lightly floured surface, roll out dough to a 20'' x 12'' rectangle, about 1 inch thick. Spread generously with Cinnamon Butter. Roll up jelly-roll fashion. Using a sharp knife, cut dough into twenty 1-inch slices. Spread Caramel Topping evenly in a 15'' x 10'' baking sheet with raised sides. Arrange slices on topping in pan, cut-side down. Cover with a damp towel. Let rise in a warm place until doubled in bulk. Preheat oven to 375°F (190°C). Bake rolls 20 to 25 minutes until golden brown. Cool on a rack 5 minutes. Invert rolls and pan onto a large platter; remove pan. Serve warm. Makes 20 large cinnamon rolls.

Cinnamon Butter:
In a small saucepan, melt butter or margarine. Over medium heat, stir in cinnamon, brown sugar, raisins and nuts. Continue stirring until sugar dissolves.

Caramel Topping:
In a small bowl, combine whipping cream, brown sugar and nuts.

Use leftover bread to make your own breadcrumbs. Process small amounts in a blender. For dry bread-cumbs, spread the crumbs out on baking sheets and dry them in the oven or on the counter.

French Bread

Use one of these whole-wheat loaves to make Savory French Onion Loaves, page 57.

1 pkg. active dry yeast (1 tablespoon)
1-1/2 cups lukewarm water (110°F, 45°C)
2 eggs, beaten
5 to 6 cups WHOLE-WHEAT
   HOT ROLL MIX, page 33

1 tablespoon cornmeal
Sesame seeds, if desired
1 to 2 tablespoons butter or margarine,
   melted

In a large bowl, stir yeast into lukewarm water until softened. Stir in eggs. Beat in 5 cups WHOLE-WHEAT HOT ROLL MIX until blended. Let rest 2 minutes. Stir in enough of the remaining mix to make a soft dough. Knead until smooth, 7 to 10 minutes. Clean and grease bowl. Place dough in bowl, turning to grease all sides. Cover with a damp towel. Let rise in a warm place, free from drafts, until doubled in bulk, about 1 hour. Generously grease 2 baking sheets. Sprinkle with cornmeal; set aside. Punch down dough. On a lightly oiled surface, divide dough into 2 balls. Roll out each ball to a 10" x 3" rectangle. Roll up firmly jelly-roll fashion, starting with one long side. Pinch to seal edges. Place rolled loaves on prepared baking sheet, seam-side down. Make 5 diagonal slashes across top of each loaf. Brush with water. Let rise until almost doubled in bulk. Preheat oven to 375°F (190°C). Brush loaves again with water. Sprinkle with sesame seeds, if desired. Place a baking pan on lower shelf of oven. Pour 1 inch warm water in pan. Place loaves on a rack in center of oven. Bake 30 to 35 minutes in preheated oven until golden brown. Brush with melted butter. Cool on a rack. Makes 2 loaves.

How to Make Whole-Wheat Cinnamon Rolls

1/With electric mixer or by hand, beat in WHOLE-WHEAT HOT ROLL MIX to make soft dough.

2/Cool rolls 5 minutes. Invert rolls and pan onto a large platter; remove pan.

Giant Braided Loaf

See the variation below for shaping the dough into pan loaves.

1 pkg. active dry yeast (1 tablespoon)
1-1/2 cups lukewarm water (110°F, 45°C)
2 eggs, beaten
1/2 cup butter or margarine, melted, or
   1/2 cup vegetable oil
5 to 6 cups WHOLE-WHEAT
   HOT ROLL MIX, page 33

1 egg yolk
1 tablespoon water
1 tablespoon caraway, sesame or poppy seeds
1 tablespoon butter or margarine, melted

In a large bowl, stir yeast into lukewarm water until softened. Stir in 2 beaten eggs and 1/2 cup melted butter or margarine or oil. Beat in 5 cups WHOLE-WHEAT HOT ROLL MIX. Let rest 2 minutes. Add enough of the remaining mix to make a soft dough. Turn out on a lightly floured surface. Knead until smooth, 7 to 10 minutes. Clean and grease bowl. Place dough in bowl, turning to grease all sides. Cover with a damp towel. Let rise in a warm place, free from drafts, until doubled in bulk. Grease 1 large baking sheet; set aside. Punch down dough. Let rest 10 minutes. Divide into 4 equal pieces. Shape 3 pieces into 15-inch ropes. Arrange ropes about 1 inch apart on greased baking sheet. Braid loosely from center to either end. Pinch ends together. Divide remaining piece of dough into 3 equal pieces. Shape each into a 12-inch rope. Braid as directed above. Place on top of large braid, pinching ends of small braid into large braid. In a small bowl, combine 1 egg yolk and 1 tablespoon water. Brush over braids. Sprinkle with caraway, sesame or poppy seeds. Cover and let rise until almost doubled in bulk. Preheat oven to 375°F (190°C). Bake 40 to 50 minutes until deep golden brown. Brush tops with 1 tablespoon melted butter or margarine. Cool on a rack. Makes 1 large loaf.

Variation

Whole-Wheat Loaves: Divide dough into 2 equal pieces. Roll out each piece into a 12" x 8" rectangle. Roll up each rectangle jelly-roll fashion, starting with a short side. Pinch ends together to seal. Place each shaped loaf in a greased 9" x 5" loaf pan, seam-side down. Cover and let rise until slightly rounded above tops of pans. Bake as directed above.

Football Hero Bun

Use this giant hamburger bun in Football Hero, page 98.

2 pkgs. active dry yeast (2 tablespoons)
3/4 cup lukewarm water (110°F, 45°C)
1 egg, beaten

1/4 cup vegetable oil
2-1/2 to 3 cups WHOLE-WHEAT
   HOT ROLL MIX, page 33

In a large bowl, stir yeast into lukewarm water until softened. Stir in egg and oil. Beat in 2-1/2 cups WHOLE-WHEAT HOT ROLL MIX. Let rest 2 minutes. Stir in enough of the remaining mix to make a soft dough. Knead until smooth, 7 to 10 minutes. Clean and grease bowl. Place dough in bowl, turning to grease all sides. Cover with a damp towel. Let rise in a warm place, free from drafts, until doubled in bulk, about 1-1/2 hours. Grease a large baking sheet; set aside. Punch down dough. Let rest 10 minutes. On a lightly oiled surface, shape dough evenly into a 9-inch circle. Place on prepared baking sheet. Let rise 10 to 15 minutes. Preheat oven to 425°F (220°C). Bake about 10 minutes until golden brown. Remove from pan; cool on a rack. Makes one 9-inch bun or 6 servings.

Giant Braided Loaf, above, is in the center. Clockwise: Swedish Rye Bread, page 107, Sopaipillas, page 101, Carrot-Orange Loaf, page 108 and Aebleskivers, page 109.

Bagels   *Photo on page 53.*

These whole-wheat bagels have a slightly pebbled surface.

2 pkgs. active dry yeast (2 tablespoons)
2 cups lukewarm water (110°F, 45°C)
5 to 5-1/2 cups WHOLE-WHEAT
   HOT ROLL MIX, page 33
Cornmeal

3 qts. water
1 tablespoon sugar
1 egg yolk, beaten
1 tablespoon water
Poppy seeds, sesame seeds or coarse salt

In a large bowl, stir yeast into 2 cups lukewarm water until softened. Beat in 4 cups WHOLE-WHEAT HOT ROLL MIX until evenly distributed. Let rest 2 minutes. Add enough of the remaining mix to make a very stiff dough. Turn out onto a lightly floured surface. Knead until smooth, 10 to 15 minutes. Add additional mix to surface as needed. Dough will be quite firm. Clean and grease bowl. Place dough in bowl, turning to grease all sides. Cover dough with a damp towel. Let rise in a warm place, free from drafts until doubled in bulk, about 1-1/2 hours. Punch down dough; knead 4 or 5 times. Divide dough into 2 equal portions. Divide each portion into 8 equal pieces. Shape each piece of dough into a smooth ball. Holding 1 ball with both hands, force your thumbs through center. With 1 thumb in the hole, shape dough like a doughnut, 3 to 3-1/2 inches across. Place bagel on lightly floured surface. Repeat with remaining dough. Cover lightly; let rise in a warm place free from drafts, 15 to 20 minutes. Lightly grease 2 baking sheets. Sprinkle with cornmeal; set aside. In a 5-quart pot, bring 3 quarts water to a boil over medium-high heat. Add sugar. Turn heat low enough to keep water boiling gently. Use a slotted spoon to carefully lower 1 bagel at a time into boiling water. Turning often, cook until slightly puffed and quite soft, about 5 minutes. Add additional water if necessary. Drain cooked bagels briefly on paper towels. Preheat oven to 400°F (205°C). Arrange bagels on prepared baking sheets with sides not touching. Combine egg yolk and 1 tablespoon water. Brush cooked bagels with egg yolk mixture. Leave plain, or sprinkle with poppy seeds, sesame seeds or coarse salt. Bake 20 to 30 minutes in preheated oven until browned. Cool on a rack. Makes 16 bagels.

Spicy Applesauce Bread

Substitute 2-1/2 teaspoons SPICE BLEND MIX, page 16, for the cinnamon, allspice and cloves.

3-3/4 cups SWEET QUICK BREAD MIX,
   page 11
2 eggs, beaten
1-1/2 teaspoons ground cinnamon
1/2 teaspoon ground allspice

1/2 teaspoon ground cloves
1 cup applesauce
1/2 cup chopped nuts
1/2 cup raisins

Preheat oven to 325°F (165°C). Grease one 9" x 5" loaf pan or two 7" x 3" loaf pans; set aside. In medium bowl, combine all ingredients, stirring to blend. Turn into prepared pan or pans. Bake 60 to 75 minutes in preheated oven until a wooden pick inserted in center comes out clean. Cool on a rack 5 minutes. Turn out of pan or pans. Cool right-side up on rack. Makes 1 or 2 loaves.

Whole-Wheat Parker House Rolls

These take a while to prepare, but are worth the effort.

1 pkg. active dry yeast (1 tablespoon)
1-1/2 cups lukewarm water (110°F, 45°C)
2 eggs, beaten
1/2 cup butter or margarine, melted, or
   1/2 cup vegetable oil

5 to 6 cups WHOLE-WHEAT
   HOT ROLL MIX, page 33
1/3 cup butter or margarine, melted

In a large bowl, stir yeast into lukewarm water until softened. Stir in eggs and 1/2 cup melted butter or margarine or oil. Beat in 5 cups WHOLE-WHEAT HOT ROLL MIX. Let rest 2 minutes. Stir in enough of the remaining mix to make a soft dough. Turn out on a lightly floured surface. Knead until smooth, 7 to 10 minutes. Clean and grease bowl. Place dough in bowl, turning to grease all sides. Cover dough with a damp towel. Let rise in a warm place, free from drafts, until doubled in bulk. Grease a large baking sheet; set aside. Roll out dough 1/2 inch thick. Cut with a floured, round biscuit cutter. Dip both sides of dough in 1/3 cup melted butter or margarine. Fold in half, stretching slightly. Arrange on prepared baking sheet, not touching. Let rise until doubled in bulk, 20 to 30 minutes. Preheat oven to 375°F (190°C). Bake 15 to 20 minutes until golden brown. Makes 24 rolls.

Variation

Pan Rolls: Grease a 13" x 9" baking pan or two 9-inch, round cake pans. Punch down dough. Divide into 24 equal pieces. Shape each piece into a smooth ball. Dip tops of each in 1/3 cup melted butter or margarine. Arrange in prepared pans, dipped side up, not touching. Cover and let rise until doubled in bulk, 20 to 30 minutes. Bake as directed above.

Swedish Rye Bread   *Photo on page 105.*

Make sandwiches with this light, beautifully textured bread.

2 pkgs. active dry yeast (2 tablespoons)
1-1/2 cups lukewarm water (110°F, 45°C)
2 eggs, beaten
1/2 cup vegetable oil or butter or
   margarine, melted
1 to 2 teaspoons caraway seeds

2 tablespoons dark molasses
3/4 cup rye flour
4 to 5 cups WHOLE-WHEAT
   HOT ROLL MIX, page 33
1 tablespoon butter or margarine, melted

In a large bowl, stir yeast into lukewarm water until softened. Stir in eggs, 1/2 cup oil, butter or margarine, caraway seeds and molasses. Beat in rye flour and 4 cups WHOLE-WHEAT HOT ROLL MIX. Let rest 2 minutes. Stir in enough of the remaining mix to make a soft dough. Knead 7 to 10 minutes until smooth. Clean and grease bowl. Place dough in bowl, turning to grease all sides. Cover with a damp towel. Let rise in a warm place, free from drafts, until doubled in bulk. Punch down dough. Let rest 10 minutes. Grease 1 large baking sheet. Divide dough in half. Shape each half into a slightly flattened ball. Arrange on prepared baking sheet. Use a sharp knife to make 2 horizontal and 2 vertical slashes on top of each loaf. Cover and let rise until about doubled in bulk. Preheat oven to 375°F (190°C). Bake 25 to 30 minutes until browned. Brush tops with 1 tablespoon melted butter or margarine. Cool on a rack. Makes 2 loaves.

Carrot-Orange Loaf   *Photo on page 105.*

When cool, serve with Cinnamon Whipped Topping from Pumpkin Bread, page 110.

3-3/4 cups SWEET QUICK BREAD MIX,
  page 11
2 eggs, beaten
1 cup grated carrots
1/2 cup orange juice

1 teaspoon grated orange peel
1 teaspoon ground nutmeg
1 teaspoon ground cinnamon
1/2 cup chopped nuts
1/2 cup raisins

Preheat oven to 325°F (165°C). Grease one 9" x 5" loaf pan or two 7" x 3" loaf pans; set aside.
In a medium bowl, combine all ingredients, stirring to blend. Turn into prepared pan or pans.
Bake 60 to 70 minutes in preheated oven until a wooden pick inserted in center comes out clean.
Cool on a rack 5 minutes. Turn out of pan. Cool right-side up on rack. Makes 1 or 2 loaves.

Variation
Substitute 1 (7-1/2-ounce) jar junior baby-food carrots for grated carrots and orange juice.

Date-Nut Bread

For a different shape, bake this bread in a Bundt pan at 325°F (165°C) for about 1 hour.

1 cup boiling water
1 cup chopped dates
2 eggs, beaten
3-3/4 cups SWEET QUICK BREAD MIX,
  page 11

1 teaspoon vanilla extract
1/2 cup chopped nuts

Preheat oven to 350°F (175°C). Grease one 9" x 5" loaf pan or two 7" x 3" loaf pans; set aside.
In a small bowl, pour boiling water over dates. Let stand 5 minutes. In a medium bowl, combine
eggs, SWEET QUICK BREAD MIX, vanilla and nuts, stirring to blend. Stir in date mixture.
Turn into prepared pan or pans. Bake 60 to 65 minutes in preheated oven until a wooden pick
inserted in center comes out clean. Cool on a rack 5 minutes. Turn out of pan or pans. Cool right-
side up on rack. Makes 1 or 2 loaves.

Banana-Nut Bread

Mash very ripe bananas with about 1 teaspoon lemon juice, then freeze and use later.

3-3/4 cups SWEET QUICK BREAD MIX,
  page 11
2 eggs, beaten

1 tablespoon lemon juice
2 medium bananas mashed (about 1 cup)
1/2 cup chopped nuts

Preheat oven to 325°F (165°C). Grease one 9" x 5" loaf pan or two 7" x 3" loaf pans; set aside.
In a medium bowl, combine all ingredients, stirring to blend. Turn into prepared pan or pans.
Bake 50 to 60 minutes in preheated oven until a wooden pick inserted in center comes out clean.
Cool on a rack 5 minutes. Turn out of pan. Cool right-side up on rack. Makes 1 or 2 loaves.

Aebleskivers *Photo on page 105.*

Aebleskivers are usually served with apple slices, apple butter or applesauce.

2 eggs, separated
1-1/2 cups BUTTERMILK PANCAKE &
WAFFLE MIX, page 8
1 cup water

2 tablespoons melted butter
Butter for frying
Powdered sugar for garnish, if desired

In a medium bowl, beat egg yolks until pale. Stir in BUTTERMILK PANCAKE & WAFFLE MIX, water and 2 tablespoons melted butter until blended. In a medium bowl, beat egg whites until stiff but not dry. Fold into egg yolk mixture. Generously butter each aebleskiver cup. Heat according to manufacturer's instructions. Fill each cup 3/4 full with batter. Cook until bubbly and set around edge, about 1-1/2 minutes. Turn 1/4 turn with a fork or wooden pick to brown other side. Continue 1/4 turns each 15 to 30 seconds until lightly browned on all sides and a wooden pick inserted in center comes out clean. Dust with powdered sugar for garnish, if desired. Serve warm. Makes about 20 aebleskivers.

Variation

After making two 1/4 turns, insert 3 or 4 fresh blueberries into unbaked portion. Continue turning and baking, enclosing berries in center.

How to Bake Aebleskivers

1/Generously butter each aebleskiver cup; heat until butter bubbles.

2/With wooden pick or fork, turn muffins 1/4 turn until browned on all sides.

Pumpkin Bread

Serve the Cinnamon Whipped Topping with any sweet quick bread.

3-3/4 cups SWEET QUICK BREAD MIX,
  page 11
1 cup mashed cooked pumpkin
2 eggs, beaten
1/2 cup milk
1/2 teaspoon ground cinnamon

1/2 teaspoon ground nutmeg
1/2 teaspoon ground cloves
1/2 cup chopped nuts
1/2 cup raisins
Cinnamon Whipped Topping, see below

Cinnamon Whipped Topping:
1 cup whipping cream
1 teaspoon ground cinnamon

3 tablespoons powdered sugar

Preheat oven to 350°F (175°C). Grease one 9" x 5" loaf pan or two 7" x 3" loaf pans; set aside. In a medium bowl, combine QUICK SWEET BREAD MIX, pumpkin, eggs, milk, cinnamon, nutmeg and cloves, stirring to blend. Stir in nuts and raisins. Turn into prepared pan or pans. Bake 55 to 60 minutes in preheated oven until a wooden pick inserted in center comes out clean. Cool on a rack 5 minutes. Turn out of pan. Prepare topping. Cool right side up on rack. To serve, cut into 1/2-inch slices; spread each with Cinnamon Whipped Topping. Makes 1 or 2 loaves.

Cinnamon Whipped Topping:
In a medium bowl, whip cream until soft peaks form. Gently stir in cinnamon and powdered sugar. Refrigerate until served. Makes about 2 cups.

Zucchini Bread

To prevent tunnels in your bread, stir only until all the indredients are moistened.

3-3/4 cups SWEET QUICK BREAD MIX,
  page 11
2 eggs, beaten
2 cups grated unpeeled zucchini squash

3 tablespoons orange juice
1 teaspoon grated orange peel
1/2 cup chopped nuts

Preheat oven to 325°F (165°C). Grease one 9" x 5" loaf pan or two 7" x 3" loaf pans; set aside. In a medium bowl, combine all ingredients, stirring to blend. Turn into prepared pan or pans. Bake 60 to 75 minutes in preheated oven until a wooden pick inserted in center comes out clean. Cool on a rack 5 minutes. Turn out of pan. Cool right-side up on rack. Makes 1 or 2 loaves.

Make your own dried grated orange or lemon peel by finely grating the peel onto waxed paper. Let it dry on the counter uncovered 3 or 4 hours.

Cranberry Bread

Freeze fresh cranberries when they are in season so you can make this bread all year.

3/4 cup orange juice
1 cup fresh or frozen cranberries
2 eggs, beaten

3-3/4 cups SWEET QUICK BREAD MIX,
  page 11
1 teaspoon grated orange peel

Preheat oven to 325°F (165°C). Grease one 9" x 5" loaf pan or two 7" x 3" loaf pans; set aside. Combine orange juice and cranberries in blender. Process on chop 4 or 5 seconds. In a medium bowl, combine eggs, SWEET QUICK BREAD MIX, orange peel and orange juice mixture, stirring to blend. Turn into prepared pan or pans. Bake 65 to 75 minutes in preheated oven until a wooden pick inserted in center comes out clean. Cool on a rack 5 minutes. Turn out of pan or pans. Cool right-side up on rack. Makes 1 or 2 loaves.

Buttermilk Waffles

All waffles should be like these—light, crisp and golden outside, tender and moist inside.

2-1/2 cups BUTTERMILK PANCAKE &
  WAFFLE MIX, page 8
2 cups water

3 eggs, separated
4 tablespoons vegetable oil

Preheat waffle baker. In a large bowl, combine BUTTERMILK PANCAKE & WAFFLE MIX, water, egg yolks and oil. Beat with a wire whisk until just blended. In a medium bowl, beat egg whites until stiff. Fold into egg yolk mixture. Bake according to waffle baker instructions. Makes 3 or 4 large waffles.

Buttermilk Pancakes

Serve these at a pancake supper with a variety of syrups.

1 egg, beaten
2 tablespoons vegetable oil
About 1 cup water, more if desired

1-1/2 cups BUTTERMILK PANCAKE &
  WAFFLE MIX, page 8

In a medium bowl, combine egg, oil and 1 cup water. With a wire whisk, stir in BUTTERMILK PANCAKE & WAFFLE MIX until blended. Let stand 5 minutes. Stir in additional water for a thinner batter. Preheat griddle according to manufacturer's directions. Lightly oil griddle. Pour about 1/3 cup batter onto hot griddle to make 1 pancake. Cook until edge is dry and bubbles form. Turn with a wide spatula. Cook 35 to 45 seconds longer until browned on both sides. Repeat with remaining batter. Makes about ten 4-inch pancakes.

Desserts

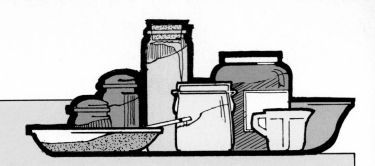

It's fun and satisfying to create desserts from scratch. You will experience this more often as you use your mixes.

No time to prepare desserts? Try the ultimate dessert convenience—SNACK CAKE MIX, page 11. Although the recipes which use this mix describe two steps for the convenience of beginners, you can mix all of the ingredients in the baking pan to save time, effort and dishwashing. Most of the cakes do not need frosting or create their own frosting while baking.

Keep several packages of FREEZER PIE CRUST MIX, page 41, in your freezer. You will have consistent success if you let it thaw completely before rolling it out. If it still contains ice crystals, the dough will be sticky and pull apart. Directions for preparing dough for single- or double-crust pies are with the mix. Graham Cracker Pie Crust will work perfectly with your favorite refrigerator pie—as well as with most of the pies in this section.

Two recipes, Lemon Light Dessert and Pineapple-Mint Dessert, require whipping partially frozen evaporated milk. Pour the milk into a small deep bowl. Place the bowl and a rotary beater or electric mixer beaters in the freezer at least 25 minutes or until ice crystals form in the milk. Whip it as you would whip cream. If the whipped milk must hold its shape longer than eight hours, *stablize* it or make it more firm by beating in 1 tablespoon lemon juice for each cup of milk used. Add 1/2 teaspoon vanilla extract to minimize the lemon taste.

If you don't like to drink milk but want the calcium it offers, the pudding and pie filling mixes contain powdered milk. Some of the recipes using these mixes are Chocolate Cream Pie, Layered Vanilla Cream, Sour Cream & Raisin Pie, Creamy Vanilla Pudding, Vanilla Cream Pie and Boston Cream Pie.

Double Chocolate Snack Cake

This moist, delicious cake frosts itself.

1 pkg. SNACK CAKE MIX, page 11
2 tablespoons unsweetened cocoa powder
3/4 cup water
1 egg
1/3 cup vegetable oil
1 teaspoon vanilla extract
1/2 cup semisweet chocolate pieces
1/2 cup chopped nuts

Preheat oven to 350°F (175°C). In an ungreased 8- or 9-inch square baking pan, combine SNACK CAKE MIX and cocoa powder. In a medium bowl, combine water, egg, oil and vanilla. Beat with a fork to blend. Stir into cocoa mixture until smooth and blended. Sprinkle chocolate pieces and nuts evenly over top of batter. Bake 30 to 40 minutes in preheated oven until surface springs back when touched with your fingers. Makes 9 servings.

Variation

Bumpy Road Snack Cake: Omit unsweetened cocoa powder. Substitute buttermilk for water.

Oatmeal Spice Cake

The topping makes this cake extra special, but it's good plain too.

3/4 cup rolled oats
1-1/4 cups boiling water
1 pkg. SNACK CAKE MIX, page 11
1 egg
1/3 cup vegetable oil
1 teaspoon ground cinnamon

1/2 teaspoon ground nutmeg
1 teaspoon vanilla extract
1/2 cup chopped nuts
1/2 cup raisins
Broiled Coconut Topping, see below

Broiled Coconut Topping:
4 tablespoons butter or margarine
1/4 cup packed brown sugar
2 tablespoons milk

1/2 teaspoon vanilla extract
1/2 cup shredded coconut
1/2 cup chopped nuts

Preheat oven to 325°F (165°C). Pour rolled oats into a small bowl. Stir in boiling water; set aside. Pour SNACK CAKE MIX into an ungreased 8- or 9-inch square baking pan; set aside. In a medium bowl, combine egg, oil, cinnamon, nutmeg and vanilla. Beat with a fork to blend. Stir in softened rolled oats mixture. Stir into SNACK CAKE MIX until blended. Stir in nuts and raisins until evenly distributed. Bake 45 minutes in preheated oven until a wooden pick inserted in center comes out clean. Prepare topping. Spread topping evenly over cake as it comes from oven. Turn oven to broil. Place cake in oven 3 inches below broiling element. Broil about 2 minutes until frosting bubbles. Makes 9 servings.

Broiled Coconut Topping:
In a small saucepan, melt butter or margarine. Stir in remaining ingredients.

Carrot Snack Cake

Substitute a 7-ounce jar of junior baby food carrots for the grated carrots and orange juice.

1 pkg. SNACK CAKE MIX, page 11
1 egg, slightly beaten
1/3 cup vegetable oil
1 cup grated carrots

3/4 cup orange juice
1 teaspoon ground cinnamon
1/2 cup chopped nuts
Cream Cheese Frosting, see below

Cream Cheese Frosting:
3 tablespoons butter or margarine, softened
1 (3-oz.) pkg. cream cheese, softened

1-2/3 cups powdered sugar, sifted
1/2 teaspoon vanilla extract

Preheat oven to 350°F (175°C). Pour SNACK CAKE MIX into an ungreased 8- or 9-inch square baking pan. In a medium bowl, combine egg, oil, carrots, orange juice and cinnamon, beating with a fork to blend. Stir into SNACK CAKE MIX until blended. Stir in nuts. Bake 35 to 45 minutes until a wooden pick inserted in center comes out clean. Prepare frosting; set aside. Cool cake on a rack. Spread frosting evenly over cooled cake. Makes 9 servings.

Cream Cheese Frosting:
In a small bowl, cream butter or margarine and cream cheese until light and fluffy. Beat in powdered sugar and vanilla until smooth.

Boston Cream Pie

In a hurry? Use Yellow Crumb Cake, page 136, for the cake base.

1-1/4 cups sifted cake flour
3/4 cup sugar
1-1/2 teaspoons baking powder
1/2 teaspoon salt
1/4 cup butter or margarine, softened
1/2 cup milk

1 teaspoon vanilla extract
2 tablespoons milk
1 egg
Cream Filling, see below
Chocolate Frosting, see below

Cream Filling:
1 egg yolk
1/3 cup VANILLA PUDDING &
  PIE FILLING MIX, page 13

1-1/4 cups milk
1 tablespoon butter or margarine
1 teaspoon vanilla extract

Chocolate Frosting:
1 cup sifted powdered sugar
2 tablespoons hot water
1 (1-oz.) square unsweetened chocolate,
  melted

1 teaspoon butter or margarine, melted

Preheat oven to 350°F (175°C). Grease and flour an 8-inch, round cake pan or a 6-inch square baking pan. In a medium bowl, combine cake flour, sugar, baking powder and salt. Stir in softened butter or margarine and 1/2 cup milk. Beat 2 minutes with an electric mixer or 5 minutes by hand. Stir in vanilla, 2 tablespoons milk and egg. Beat 2 minutes longer. Pour batter into prepared pan. Bake 30 minutes in preheated oven until cake is lightly browned and a wooden pick inserted in center comes out clean. Cool on a rack. Use a knife with a long thin blade to cut cake in half horizontally. Prepare Cream Filling; let cool. Prepare Chocolate Frosting; set aside. Place bottom layer of split cake on a 10-inch, round platter. Spread cooled filling evenly over bottom cake layer. Gently place top layer of split cake on top of filling. Spread frosting over top layer. Refrigerate 3 to 4 hours. Makes 8 servings.

Cream Filling:
In a small bowl, lightly beat egg yolk; set aside. In a small saucepan, combine VANILLA PUDDING & PIE FILLING MIX and milk. Cook and stir over medium heat until mixture thickens and begins to bubble, 3 to 5 minutes. Stirring vigorously, pour about half of hot milk mixture into beaten egg yolk. Slowly stir egg mixture into remaining hot milk mixture. Cook and stir 1 minute longer. Remove from heat. Stir in butter or margarine and vanilla until blended. Cover with plastic wrap; cool on a rack.

Chocolate Frosting:
In a medium bowl, combine powdered sugar and water. Beat in chocolate and butter or margarine until smooth.

Whip 1 cup whipping cream to get 2 cups whipped cream.

Party Trifle

This elegant but simple dessert will serve a large group.

Lemon Pound Cake, page 135
1/2 cup orange juice
Creamy Vanilla Pudding, page 126
3 pints fresh strawberries

1 cup cubed fresh pineapple or
  canned pineapple chunks, if desired
2 cups sweetened whipped cream
1 cup chopped walnuts, if desired

Cut cake into 1-inch cubes. Place 1/2 of the cake cubes in a deep 3-quart glass bowl. Sprinkle with 1/2 of the orange juice. Spoon about 1/2 of the Creamy Vanilla Pudding over cake; set aside. Rinse strawberries, reserving 6 or 8 for garnish. Hull remaining strawberries. In a medium bowl, combine hulled strawberries and pineapple, if desired. Spread half of fruit mixture over pudding-coated cake. Spread half of whipped cream over fruit. Sprinkle with nuts. Repeat layers of cake, orange juice, pudding, fruit and whipped cream. Garnish with reserved strawberries. Refrigerate 4 hours or overnight. To serve, spoon into dessert bowls. Makes 12 to 15 servings.

How to Make Boston Cream Pie

1/Insert wooden picks around center side of cake. Use picks as guide to cut cake horizontally.

2/Spread filling between cake layers. Spread glaze over top of cake.

Banana-Walnut Snack Cake

Place a paper doily on the hot cake, dust with powdered sugar, then remove the doily.

1 pkg. SNACK CAKE MIX, page 11	**1/2 cup mashed ripe banana**
1 egg	**1/2 cup buttermilk, milk or water**
1/3 cup vegetable oil	**1/2 cup chopped walnuts**

Preheat oven to 350°F (175°C). Pour SNACK CAKE MIX into an ungreased 8- or 9-inch square baking pan. In a small bowl, combine remaining ingredients, beating with a fork to blend. Stir into SNACK CAKE MIX until blended. Bake 30 to 35 minutes in preheated oven until a wooden pick inserted in center comes out clean. Cool on a rack. Makes 9 servings.

Applesauce Snack Cake

Substitute 2-1/2 teaspoons SPICE BLEND MIX, page 16, for the cinnamon, allspice and cloves.

1 pkg. SNACK CAKE MIX, page 11	**1/2 teaspoon ground allspice**
1 egg	**1/8 teaspoon ground cloves**
1/3 cup vegetable oil	**1/2 cup chopped nuts**
3/4 cup applesauce	**1 cup raisins**
1-1/2 teaspoons ground cinnamon	

Preheat oven to 325°F (165°C). Pour SNACK CAKE MIX into an ungreased 8- or 9-inch square baking pan; set aside. In a small bowl, combine egg, oil, applesauce, cinnamon, allspice and cloves, beating with a fork to blend. Stir into SNACK CAKE MIX until smooth and blended. Stir in nuts and raisins. Bake 35 to 45 minutes until a wooden pick inserted in center comes out clean. Cool on a rack. Makes 6 servings.

Fresh Peach Pie

When they are in season, use fresh strawberries instead of peaches.

Single Freezer Pie Crust, baked, page 41	**1/4 cup water**
1 cup fresh peaches, crushed	**1 tablespoon lemon juice**
1/3 cup water	**1 tablespoon butter or margarine**
1 cup sugar	**3 to 4 cups sliced fresh peaches**
4 tablespoons cornstarch	**2 cups sweetened whipped cream for garnish**
Pinch salt	

Prepare pie crust in a 9-inch pie plate; set aside to cool. In a medium saucepan, combine 1 cup crushed peaches and 1/3 cup water. Stir constantly over medium heat until mixture begins to boil. Cook and stir about 2 minutes longer. Remove from heat. In a medium bowl, combine sugar, cornstarch, salt, 1/4 cup water and lemon juice, beating with a wire whisk to blend. Stir into cooked peach mixture. Cook and stir over medium heat until slightly thickened. Stir in butter or margarine until blended. Set aside to cool. Arrange 3 to 4 cups sliced peaches in prepared pie crust. Spoon cooled mixture over peaches. Refrigerate 2 hours. To serve, cut in wedges. Garnish each wedge with a dollop of sweetened whipped cream. Makes about 8 servings.

Sour Cream & Raisin Pie

To change the pie, top it with Mile High Meringue from Sour Cream & Lemon Pie, below.

Single Freezer Pie Crust, baked, page 41
2/3 cup VANILLA PUDDING &
  PIE FILLING MIX, page 13
2-1/2 cups milk
1/4 teaspoon ground nutmeg
1/4 teaspoon ground cinnamon

1/3 cup raisins
2 tablespoons butter or margarine
1 teaspoon vanilla extract
1 cup dairy sour cream
2 cups sweetened whipped cream

Prepare pie crust in a 9-inch pie plate; set aside to cool. In a medium saucepan, combine VANILLA PUDDING & PIE FILLING MIX, milk, nutmeg, cinnamon and raisins. Cook and stir over medium heat until mixture thickens and begins to bubble, 3 to 5 minutes. Remove from heat. Stir in butter or margarine and vanilla until blended. Cover with plastic wrap. Cool on a rack. Fold in sour cream. Pour into baked pie crust. Top with sweetened whipped cream. Makes about 8 servings.

Sour Cream & Lemon Pie

This meringue won't stick to your fork as you eat it.

Single Freezer Pie Crust, baked, page 41
1 cup sugar
5 tablespoons cornstarch
Pinch salt
1 cup milk
3 egg yolks

4 tablespoons butter or margarine
1 teaspoon lemon peel
1/3 cup fresh lemon juice
1 cup dairy sour cream
Mile-High Meringue, see below

Mile-High Meringue:
1 tablespoon cornstarch
3 tablespoons sugar
Pinch salt
1 teaspoon lemon juice

1/2 cup water
3 egg whites, room temperature
6 tablespoons sugar

Prepare pie crust in a 9-inch pie plate; set aside to cool. In a small saucepan, combine sugar, cornstarch and salt. Gradually stir in milk. Cook and stir over medium heat until smooth and slightly thickened; set aside. In a small bowl, beat egg yolks with a wire whisk. Beating vigorously, add about half of hot mixture. Slowly stir egg mixture into remaining hot mixture. Cook and stir 2 minutes; set aside. Stir in butter or margarine, lemon peel and lemon juice. Cover with plastic wrap. Cool on a rack. Fold in sour cream. Pour into prepared pie crust; set aside. Prepare Mile-High Meringue. Preheat oven to 325°F (165°C). Spoon meringue on top of pie, spreading to seal completely. Bake 30 minutes in preheated oven until golden brown. Makes about 8 servings.

Mile-High Meringue:
In a small saucepan, combine cornstarch, 3 tablespoons sugar, salt, lemon juice and water. Cook and stir over medium heat until clear and thickened. Set aside to cool. In a large bowl, beat egg whites until soft peaks form. Gradually add cooled cornstarch mixture, beating until mixture thickens. Gradually add 6 tablespoons sugar, beating until soft peaks form, 5 to 8 minutes.

Queen Pie

Drain the maraschino cherries on paper towels before you use them as a garnish.

Single Freezer Pie Crust, baked, page 41
1 egg, slightly beaten
1 cup powdered sugar
1/4 cup butter or margarine, softened
1/8 teaspoon salt
1/4 teaspoon vanilla extract
1-1/2 cups whipping cream

2/3 cup crushed pineapple, well-drained
1/4 cup chopped maraschino cherries,
  well-drained
1/4 cup chopped pecans
Maraschino cherry halves for garnish
Mint sprigs for garnish

Prepare pie crust in a 9-inch pie plate; set aside to cool. In a small bowl, combine egg, powdered sugar, butter or margarine, salt and vanilla. Beat with an electric mixer until light and creamy. Spread evenly in baked pie crust. In a medium bowl, whip cream until soft peaks form. Fold in well-drained pineappple, well-drained chopped maraschino cherries and pecans. Spread evenly over powdered sugar mixture. Refrigerate 2 hours. Garnish with maraschino cherry halves and mint sprigs. Makes about 8 servings.

Variation

Substitute 1/2 cup sliced strawberries for pineapple.

Cherry-Almond Pie

For special occasions, make a lattice-top crust by weaving strips of dough.

2 (1-lb.) cans pitted sour pie cherries
1-1/4 cups sugar
1/3 cup all-purpose flour
1/4 teaspoon salt
1 tablespoon butter or margarine, melted

1/4 teaspoon almond extract
1/4 teaspoon red food coloring, if desired
Double Freezer Pie Crust, unbaked,
  page 41
Almond Glaze, see below

Almond Glaze:
1 cup powdered sugar
1/2 teaspoon almond extract

About 2 tablespoons cream or milk

Drain cherries, reserving 1/2 cup juice. In a medium bowl, combine cherries, sugar, flour, salt, butter or margarine, almond extract, 1/2 cup reserved cherry juice and food coloring, if desired. Let stand about 10 minutes. Preheat oven to 425°F (220°C). Prepare bottom pie crust in a 9-inch pie plate. Pour cherry mixture into unbaked crust. Cover with top crust. Cut slits in top crust to let steam escape. Trim and flute edges. Bake about 40 minutes in preheated oven until evenly browned. Prepare glaze. Brush top of hot pie with Almond Glaze. Makes about 8 servings.

Almond Glaze:

In a small bowl, combine powdered sugar, almond extract and enough cream or milk to make a thin mixture.

Chocolate Cream Pie

Make Chocolate Banana Cream Pie by slicing 2 bananas into the baked pie crust.

Single Freezer Pie Crust, baked, page 41
1 cup CHOCOLATE PUDDING &
  PIE FILLING MIX, page 15
2-1/2 cups milk

2 tablespoons butter or margarine
1 teaspoon vanilla extract
2 cups sweetened whipped cream, if desired

Prepare pie crust in a 9-inch pie plate; set aside to cool. In a medium saucepan, combine CHOCO-LATE PUDDING & PIE FILLING MIX and milk. Cook and stir over medium heat until mixture thickens and begins to bubble, 3 to 5 minutes. Cook and stir 1 minute longer. Remove from heat. Stir in butter or margarine and vanilla until blended. Cool slightly. Pour into pie crust; cover with plastic wrap. Refrigerate 2 to 3 hours. To serve, top with sweetened whipped cream, if desired. Makes about 8 servings.

Ice Cream Sundae Pie

In a springform pan, press the crust over the bottom and about 2-1/2 inches up the side.

1-1/2 cups CHOCOLATE WAFER CRUST
  MIX, page 14
1/4 cup butter or margarine, melted
1/2 gal. peppermint or vanilla ice cream,
  slightly softened

1-1/2 cups Quick Fudge Sauce, page 123
1 cup chopped nuts
2 cups sweetened whipped cream for garnish
1/2 cup crushed peppermint candy
  for garnish

In a small bowl, combine CHOCOLATE WAFER CRUST MIX and butter or margarine. Press crumb mixture over bottom and up side of a 10-inch pie plate. Spoon half of ice cream into crust. With a large spoon make several indentions in ice cream. Spoon half of the fudge sauce into indentions. Sprinkle with half of the nuts. Repeat layers. Cover with plastic wrap. Freeze until very firm, 2 to 4 hours. To serve, cut in wedges. Garnish each wedge with sweetened whipped cream and crushed peppermint candy. Makes 8 to 10 servings.

Chocolate Wafer Pie Crust

Also use the crumb mixture to sprinkle over puddings or pies.

1-1/4 cups CHOCOLATE WAFER CRUST
  MIX, page 14

1/4 cup butter or margarine, melted

If baking crust, preheat oven to 375°F (190°C). In a medium bowl, combine CHOCOLATE WAFER CRUST MIX and melted butter or margarine. Press firmly over bottom and up side of a 9-inch pie plate. Refrigerate pie crust 45 minutes before filling, or bake 6 to 8 minutes in pre-heated oven; cool completely before adding filling. Makes one 9-inch crust.

Vanilla Cream Pie

This creamy pie filling has no eggs in it.

Single Freezer Pie Crust, baked, page 41
2/3 cup VANILLA PUDDING &
  PIE FILLING MIX, page 13

2-1/2 cups milk
2 tablespoons butter or margarine
1-1/2 teaspoons vanilla extract

Prepare crust in a 9-inch pie plate; set aside to cool. In a medium saucepan, combine VANILLA PUDDING & PIE FILLING MIX and milk. Cook and stir over medium heat until mixture thickens and begins to bubble, 3 to 5 minutes. Remove from heat. Stir in butter or margarine and vanilla until blended. Cover with plastic wrap. Cool on a rack. Pour into baked pie crust. Refrigerate about 2 hours. Makes about 8 servings.

Variations

Banana Cream Pie: Slice 2 ripe bananas into pie crust before adding filling.
Strawberry Cream Pie: Stir 2 to 4 tablespoons sugar into 2 cups sliced strawberries. Let stand 1 hour. Drain off juice. Spoon sweetened strawberries into baked pie crust. Pour chilled filling over strawberries. Top with 2 cups sweetened whipped cream.
Coconut Cream Pie: Fold 3/4 cup shredded coconut into cooled filling. Garnish with sweetened whipped cream and 1/4 cup toasted shredded coconut.

Triple Chocolate Pie

Chocolate crust, chocolate filling and chocolate topping—who could ask for more!

Chocolate Wafer Pie Crust, unbaked,
  opposite page
3 (1-oz.) squares semisweet chocolate
4 (3-oz.) pkgs. cream cheese, softened

3/4 cup sugar
2 eggs
1/2 cup dairy sour cream, room temperature
1 teaspoon vanilla extract

Topping:
2 (1-oz.) squares semisweet chocolate
1/2 cup dairy sour cream, room temperature

Prepare crust in a 9-inch pie plate. Refrigerate 1 hour. Melt chocolate; set aside to cool. Preheat oven to 350°F (175°C). In a large bowl, beat cream cheese and sugar until creamy. Beat in eggs one at a time until blended. Stir sour cream into cooled chocolate. Beat chocolate mixture and vanilla into egg mixture until smooth. Spoon into prepared crust. Bake 40 to 45 minutes in preheated oven until filling is firm. Turn off oven. Let pie cool in oven with door ajar, about 1 hour. Surface of pie will crack. Prepare Topping; cool on a rack. When thoroughly cooled, spread topping evenly over pie. Refrigerate 3 to 4 hours until firm. Makes 8 to 10 servings.

Topping:
Melt chocolate over boiling water; set aside to cool slightly. Stir in sour cream until smooth.

Melt chocolate over hot water to keep it from burning or separating.

Layered Chocolate & Vanilla Dessert

You can also use Graham Cracker Pie Crust, next page, with this dessert.

1 cup butter or margarine
1 cup finely chopped nuts
1 cup all-purpose flour
1 cup powdered sugar
1 (8-oz.) pkg. cream cheese, softened
1 cup whipping cream, whipped

Creamy Vanilla Pudding, and variation
   Creamy Chocolate Pudding,
   page 126, chilled
2 cups sweetened whipped cream, if desired
1/2 cup shredded coconut, if desired

Preheat oven to 325°F (165°C). In a medium bowl, combine butter or margarine, nuts and flour until crumbly. Press into bottom of a 13" x 9" baking pan. Bake for 25 to 30 minutes in preheated oven until lightly browned. Cool on a rack. In a medium bowl, combine powdered sugar and cream cheese, beating until smooth. Fold in whipped cream. Carefully pour over prepared crust. Spread chocolate pudding evenly over cream cheese mixture and vanilla pudding over chocolate pudding. Garnish with sweetened whipped cream and coconut, if desired. Makes about 15 servings.

Layered Vanilla Cream

You'll like this French-style dessert as much as we do.

1-1/4 cups VANILLA PUDDING &
   PIE FILLING MIX, page 13
3-2/3 cups milk
3 tablespoons butter or margarine

1-1/2 teaspoons vanilla extract
Chocolate Glaze Topping, see below
1 cup whipping cream
45 single graham crackers (do not crush)

Chocolate Glaze Topping:
2 (1-oz.) squares semisweet chocolate
6 tablespoons butter or margarine
2 tablespoons white corn syrup

2 teaspoons vanilla extract
1-1/2 cups powdered sugar
3 tablespoons milk

In a medium saucepan, combine VANILLA PUDDING & PIE FILLING MIX and milk. Cook and stir over medium heat until mixture begins to bubble, 3 to 5 minutes. Remove from heat. Stir in butter or margarine and vanilla until blended. Cover with plastic wrap. Cool on a rack. Prepare topping; set aside. In a large bowl, whip cream until stiff peaks form. Fold into cooled pudding mixture. Arrange 15 single graham crackers in bottom of a 13" x 9" baking dish. Spread half of pudding mixture over crackers. Repeat layers. Arrange remaining 15 single graham crackers on top. Pour Chocolate Glaze Topping over top layer of crackers. Cover with plastic wrap. Refrigerate at least 10 hours. Makes 12 servings.

Chocolate Glaze Topping:
In a small saucepan, melt chocolate and butter or margarine. Stir in corn syrup, vanilla, powdered sugar and milk, beating until smooth.

Chocolate-Marshmallow Dessert

If you don't like almonds, use a plain chocolate bar.

**1-1/2 cups GRAHAM CRACKER CRUST
  MIX, page 15**
1/3 cup melted butter or margarine
32 large marshmallows

1 (8-oz.) almond chocolate bar
1/2 cup milk
1 cup whipping cream, whipped
1/4 teaspoon almond extract

In a small bowl, combine GRAHAM CRACKER CRUST MIX and melted butter or margarine. Press 1 cup of mixture into bottom of a 9-inch square baking pan; set aside. In top of a double boiler, combine marshmallows, chocolate bar and milk. Stir over simmering water until marshmallows and chocolate are melted. Set aside to cool. Fold in whipped cream and almond extract. Spread mixture evenly over crust in pan. Sprinkle remaining crust mix over filling. Refrigerate 3 to 4 hours. Makes about 9 servings.

Graham Cracker Pie Crust

With the crust so easy to make, you'll be tempted to make sweet pies more often.

**1-1/2 cups GRAHAM CRACKER CRUST
  MIX, page 15**

1/3 cup butter or margarine, melted

If baking crust, preheat oven to 375°F (190°C). In a medium bowl, combine GRAHAM CRACKER CRUST MIX and melted butter or margarine. Press firmly over bottom and up side of a 9-inch pie plate. Refrigerate 45 minutes before filling, or bake 6 to 8 minutes in preheated oven; cool completely before adding filling. Fill as desired. Makes one 9-inch crust.

Quick Fudge Sauce

Stir continuously over low heat to prevent the mixture from scorching or lumping.

**1-1/2 cups CHOCOLATE SYRUP MIX,
  page 27**

6 tablespoons butter or margarine

In a small saucepan, combine Chocolate Syrup Mix and butter or margarine. Cook and stir over low heat until smooth, thick and shiny, 5 to 10 minutes. Makes about 1-1/2 cups.

Pineapple-Mint Dessert

Place the bowl, evaporated milk and beaters in the freezer about 25 minutes before using them.

2 cups CHOCOLATE WAFER CRUST
  MIX, page 14
1/4 cup butter or margarine, melted
1 (20-oz.) can crushed pineapple
1 (3-oz.) pkg. lime gelatin
1 (8-oz.) pkg. cream cheese, softened

1 cup powdered sugar
Chocolate Glaze, see below
2/3 cup evaporated milk, partially frozen
1/2 teaspoon peppermint extract
Fresh mint sprigs, if desired

Chocolate Glaze:
1/2 cup chocolate pieces
1/3 cup evaporated milk

1 tablespoon butter or margarine
1/4 teaspoon peppermint extract

Preheat oven to 375°F (190°C). In a small bowl, combine CHOCOLATE WAFER CRUST MIX and melted butter or margarine. Press into bottom of a 13" x 9" baking pan. Bake 6 to 8 minutes in preheated oven. Set aside to cool. Drain juice from pineapple into a small saucepan, pressing to remove as much juice as possible. Bring pineapple juice to a boil over medium-high heat. Remove from heat; stir in gelatin until dissolved. Set aside to cool. In a medium bowl, beat cream cheese and powdered sugar until light and fluffy. Stir in cooled gelatin mixture and drained pineapple. Refrigerate 30 to 45 minutes until thick but not set. Prepare Chocolate Glaze; set aside. Using an electric mixer or a wire whisk, beat chilled evaporated milk until soft peaks form. Beat in peppermint extract. Fold into gelatin mixture. Pour into baked crust. Drizzle glaze over gelatin mixture. Cut into squares; serve on dessert plates with a sprig of fresh mint, if desired.

Chocolate Glaze:
In a small saucepan, combine chocolate pieces, evaporated milk, butter or margarine and peppermint extract. Stir constantly over medium heat until blended.

Lemon Light Dessert

This refreshing dessert goes well with a meat and potato meal.

3 eggs, beaten
6 tablespoons lemon juice
Grated peel of 1 lemon
  (about 1-1/2 teaspoons)
3/4 cup sugar

1-1/2 cups GRAHAM CRACKER CRUST
  MIX, page 15
1 (13-oz.) can evaporated milk,
  partially frozen

In top of double boiler, combine eggs, lemon juice, lemon peel and sugar. Cook and stir over hot water until thickened. Cool on a rack. Spread 1 cup of the GRAHAM CRACKER CRUST MIX in bottom of an ungreased 11" by 7" baking pan. In a large bowl, whip chilled evaporated milk until thick. Fold into cooled lemon mixture. Spoon evenly over crumbs in pan. Sprinkle remaining GRAHAM CRACKER CRUST MIX over filling. Refrigerate 3 to 4 hours. To serve, cut in 12 rectangles. Makes 12 servings.

For a quick garnish on puddings, freeze dollops of whipped cream on a baking sheet. Store them in a plastic bag or in a plastic freezer container with a tight-fitting lid.

Chocolate-Peppermint Supreme

Use your blender to crush the peppermint candy.

1/2 cup butter or margarine, softened
1 cup powdered sugar
3 eggs, separated, room temperature
1 (1-oz.) square unsweetened chocolate,
   melted
1/2 cup chopped nuts
1-1/2 cups GRAHAM CRACKER CRUST
   MIX, page 15

1 cup whipping cream
1 (3-oz.) pkg. hard peppermint candy,
   crushed
1/2 cup miniature marshmallows
1/2 cup chopped nuts

In a medium bowl, cream butter or margarine and powdered sugar. Beat in egg yolks. Stir in melted chocolate and 1/2 cup nuts. In a medium bowl, beat egg whites until soft peaks form. Fold into chocolate mixture; set aside. Spread 3/4 cup of the GRAHAM CRACKER CRUST MIX in bottom of an 8-inch square baking pan. Spoon chocolate mixture over crumbs. Refrigerate 1 hour. Whip cream until stiff peaks form. Fold in peppermint candy, marshmallows and 1/2 cup nuts. Spoon evenly over chilled chocolate mixture. Sprinkle with remaining 3/4 cup of the GRAHAM CRACKER CRUST MIX. Refrigerate at least 1 hour. Makes about 12 servings.

How to Make Pineapple-Mint Dessert

1/Gently fold whipped evaporated milk into gelatin-pineapple mixture.

2/Drizzle or spread Chocolate Glaze over chilled gelatin mixture.

Chocolate Chip Ice Cream

Because imitation vanilla looses strength when frozen, use genuine vanilla extract.

4 eggs
2 cups sugar
2 tablespoons vanilla extract
Pinch salt

3/4 cup CHOCOLATE SYRUP MIX, page 27
1 (6-oz.) pkg. chocolate pieces
2 qts. half and half
2 (13-oz.) cans evaporated milk

In a blender, process eggs, sugar, vanilla and salt on high speed about 15 seconds. Add CHOCO-LATE SYRUP MIX and chocolate pieces. Blend on high until chocolate pieces are finely broken. Pour into metal ice cream freezer container. Stir in half and half and evaporated milk until evenly distributed. Freeze according to manufacturer's directions. Makes about 4 quarts ice cream.

Creamy Vanilla Pudding

Omit the egg yolks if you prefer a lighter pudding.

2 egg yolks
2/3 cup VANILLA PUDDING &
   PIE FILLING MIX, page 13

2-3/4 cups milk
2 tablespoons butter or margarine
1-1/2 teaspoons vanilla extract

In a medium bowl, beat egg yolks; set aside. In a medium saucepan, combine VANILLA PUD-DING & PIE FILLING MIX and milk. Cook and stir over medium heat until mixture thickens and begins to bubble. Stirring vigorously, pour about half of the hot mixture into beaten egg yolks. Stir egg yolk mixture into remaining hot mixture. Cook and stir 1 minute longer. Remove from heat. Stir in butter or margarine and vanilla until blended. Pour cooked pudding into 6 dessert or custard cups. Cover each with plastic wrap. Refrigerate 1 hour. Makes 6 servings.

Variation

Creamy Chocolate Pudding: Omit egg yolks. Substitute 1 cup CHOCOLATE PUDDING & PIE FILLING MIX, page 15, for VANILLA PUDDING & PIE FILLING MIX.

Chocolate Ice Cream Soda

You're sure to enjoy this flavor combination.

1/4 cup milk
3 tablespoons CHOCOLATE SYRUP MIX,
   page 27

2 scoops vanilla or chocolate ice cream
1 to 1-1/2 cups gingerale, club soda or
   lemon-lime soda

Combine milk and CHOCOLATE SYRUP MIX in a tall 16-ounce glass. Stir with an iced-tea spoon to blend. Add 1 scoop ice cream and 1/2 cup soda. Stir to soften ice cream. Add remaining scoop of ice cream. Pour additional soda to top of glass. Serve immediately. Makes 1 serving.

Chocolate Filled Pirouette Cookies

Dip one end of each filled cookie in melted chocolate then in finely chopped nuts.

Chocolate Cream Pie filling, page 120
2 (5-1/2-oz.) boxes pirouette cookies

Spoon cooled filling into a pastry tube with a small round tip. Using gentle pressure, squeeze mixture evenly into each cookie. Return cookies to original box. Wrap box in foil; refrigerate at least 1 hour or freeze up to 1 month. Makes 48 filled cookies.

Variations

Vanilla Filled Pirouette Cookies: Substitute Vanilla Cream Pie filling, page 121, for Chocolate Cream Pie filling.

Black & White Pirouette Cookies: Combine 1/2 cup whipping cream, whipped, 1 (3-ounce) package softened cream cheese and 2 tablespoons powdered sugar. Fill half of each cookie with cream cheese mixture. Complete filling cookies with Chocolate Cream Pie filling.

Chocolate Cream Cakes

For plain, soft chocolate cookies, eliminate the filling.

5 cups BUTTERMILK COOKIE MIX,
  page 10
2/3 cup unsweetened cocoa powder
1-1/2 cups water

2 eggs
1 teaspoon vanilla extract
Creamy Filling, see below

Creamy Filling:
1/2 cup milk
2 tablespoons all-purpose flour
1/4 cup vegetable shortening

1/4 cup butter or margarine, softened
1/2 cup sugar
1 teaspoon vanilla extract

Lightly grease 2 large baking sheets; set aside. Preheat oven to 375°F (190°C). In a large bowl, combine BUTTERMILK COOKIE MIX and cocoa powder, stirring until evenly distributed. Beat in water, eggs and vanilla until smooth. Drop onto prepared baking sheets by tablespoons. Bake 8 to 10 minutes in preheated oven until cookies are set. Cool on wire racks. Prepare Creamy Filling. Spread on bottoms of cooled cookies. Sandwich 2 cookies with filling between. Repeat with remaining cookies. Makes 24 cookie sandwiches or 48 single cookies.

Creamy Filling:
In a small saucepan, combine milk and flour, stirring over medium heat until mixture thickens. Set aside to cool. In a medium bowl, combine shortening, butter or margarine, sugar and vanilla, beating with electric mixer until light and creamy. Add cooled flour mixture; continue beating 5 minutes longer.

Variation

Chocolate Sundae Cookies: Omit Creamy Filling. Cut 24 large marshmallows in half with scissors. As cookies come from oven, place 1/2 marshmallow, cut side down, on each warm cookie. Return to oven 1 minute. With back of a spoon, press down lightly on each marshmallow to spread. Cool on a rack. Frost with Chocolate Buttercream Frosting, a variation on page 13. Top each with 1 walnut half. Makes 48 cookies.

Carrot Cookies

Even if you don't like carrots, you'll love these cookies.

1 egg, slightly beaten
1/2 cup water
1 teaspoon vanilla extract
1 teaspoon grated orange peel
1/3 cup grated carrots

1/4 cup shredded coconut
1/4 cup raisins, if desired
2-1/2 cups BUTTERMILK COOKIE
   MIX, page 10

Golden Glow Frosting:
1 cup powdered sugar
1 tablespoon orange juice
1 to 2 drops orange food coloring,
   if desired

1 tablespoon butter or margarine, softened
1/2 teaspoon vanilla extract

Lightly grease a large baking sheet; set aside. Preheat oven to 400°F (205°C). In a large bowl, combine egg, water, vanilla, orange peel, carrots, coconut and raisins, if desired. Stir in BUTTERMILK COOKIE MIX until blended. Drop by tablespoons onto prepared baking sheet. Bake 8 to 10 minutes in preheated oven until softly set and lightly browned around edges. Prepare Golden Glow Frosting. Spread over cooled cookies. Makes 18 cookies.

Golden Glow Frosting:
In a small bowl, combine all ingredients.

Cinnamon Jumbos

The batter will be more like cake batter than cookie dough.

2 tablespoons sugar
1/2 teaspoon ground cinnamon
1 egg
1/2 cup water

1 teaspoon vanilla extract
2-1/2 cups BUTTERMILK COOKIE
   MIX, page 10

Lightly grease a large baking sheet; set aside. In a small bowl, combine sugar and cinnamon; set aside. Preheat oven to 400°F (205°C). In a large bowl, combine egg, water and vanilla. Stir in BUTTERMILK COOKIE MIX until blended. Drop by tablespoons onto prepared baking sheet. Sprinkle generously with sugar-cinnamon mixture. Bake 8 to 10 minutes in preheated oven until softly set and lightly browned around edges. Cool on a rack. Makes 18 cookies.

Variations
Soft Chocolate Chip Cookies: Fold 1 cup chocolate pieces into dough. Omit sugar-cinnamon mixture.
Iced Vanilla Cookies: Omit sugar-cinnamon mixture. Frost with 1/2 recipe Vanilla Buttercream Frosting, page 13.
Candy Treat Cookies: Gently fold 1/2 to 3/4 cup small candy-coated chocolates into dough. Omit sugar-cinnamon mixture.
Boiled Raisin Cookies: Boil 3/4 cup raisins in 1 cup water. Drain, reserving liquid. Substitute 1/2 cup reserved liquid for water. Fold boiled raisins and 1/2 teaspoon nutmeg into dough.

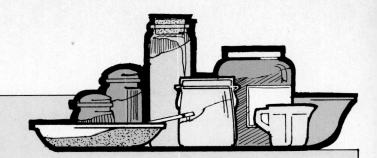

Small Families

The mix-it-yourself concept often creates the image of large quantity cooking. The time, money and energy saved by making your own mixes are evident for someone preparing meals for a family of eight. However, these same advantages are enjoyed by singles and small family households.

When cooking small quantities, saucepans, baking and mixing equipment should also be small. You should have 1- and 2-quart saucepans, 1-quart casserole dishes, 5'' x 3'' and 7'' x 3'' loaf pans, 9-inch pie plates, muffin pans and at least one 6-1/2-inch square baking pan.

Small Family Pantry Mixes, page 21, and *Small Family Freezer Mixes,* page 47, follow master mixes in the pantry mix and freezer mix sections. Some basic and high-health mixes are sized for small families. However, most recipes using those mixes serve four to six people. You can quickly modify them to provide the number of servings you need.

Heating a full-size oven for one or two baked potatoes or a small meat loaf wastes fuel and money. Cook your entire meal—appetizer, entree, side dish and dessert—at the same time. If time allows, bake tart shells, a cake from CRUMB CAKE MIX, page 23, SLICE & BAKE SUGAR COOKIES, page 42, a quick bread or muffins. Cool, wrap in moisture-vapor-proof paper or heavy-duty foil and store these pre-cooked foods in your freezer to enjoy later.

All-purpose QUICK MIX, page 21, can be used in any recipe in any book that calls for biscuit mix. Or, use it with over 30 recipes from our first book, *Make-A-Mix Cookery.*

You'll find the recipes using SPAGHETTI SEASONING MIX, page 22, CHICKEN CONTINENTAL RICE MIX, page 22, and CHILI SEASONING MIX, page 21, with the mixes rather than in this section. These out-of-the-ordinary mixes serve two people.

Casserole Pizza

For variety, prepare this delicious pie in a 9-inch pie pan.

1/2 cup tomato sauce
1/4 teaspoon dried oregano leaves, crushed
1/8 teaspoon dried sweet basil leaves,
   crushed
1 (4-oz.) can sliced mushrooms, drained
1 pkg. MEAT LOAF MIX,
   page 48, thawed

6 green pepper rings
1 cup shredded mozzarella cheese (4 oz.)
1 tablespoon grated Romano cheese
Sliced black ripe olives for garnish
2 parsley sprigs for garnish

In a medium bowl, combine tomato sauce, oregano, basil and mushrooms; set aside. Preheat oven to 375°F (190°C). Turn MEAT LOAF MIX evenly into two 4-inch pie pans, ramekins or individual casserole dishes. Spoon tomato sauce mixture evenly over mix. Bake 15 minutes in preheated oven. Remove from oven and top each with 3 green pepper rings. Sprinkle evenly with mozzarella cheese and Romano cheese. Bake 10 minutes longer. Garnish with black olives and parsley sprigs. Makes 2 servings.

Meat Loaf Tarts

Serve this piquant sauce with any mild-flavored meat.

Tangy Topper Sauce, see below
1 pkg. MEAT LOAF MIX, page 48, thawed

Tangy Topper Sauce:
1/4 cup ketchup
2 tablespoons packed brown sugar

1/4 teaspoon ground nutmeg
1/2 teaspoon dry mustard

Prepare Tangy Topper Sauce; set aside. Preheat oven to 350°F (175°C). Grease a 5" x 3" loaf pan or 2 tart pans. Shape MEAT LOAF MIX into prepared pan or pans. Spread Tangy Topper Sauce over meat. Bake 35-to 40 minutes in preheated oven until browned. Makes 2 servings.

Tangy Topper Sauce:
In a small bowl, combine all ingredients.

Meat Loaf Wellington

Plan ahead. This meat loaf must cool before you wrap it in pastry.

1 pkg. MEAT LOAF MIX,
  page 48, thawed
1 (9" x 5") sheet frozen puff pastry,
  thawed

1 egg yolk, beaten

Preheat oven to 350°F (175°C). Grease a 5" x 3" loaf pan. Press MEAT LOAF MIX into prepared pan. Bake 30 minutes until browned. Turn off oven. Cool meat loaf on a rack about 30 minutes. Cut two 12-inch pieces plastic wrap. Dust each lightly with flour. Roll puff pastry between lightly floured plastic wrap to a 9" x 8" rectangle. Remove top plastic wrap; discard. Invert pastry onto a small baking sheet. Remove remaining plastic wrap. Place cooled meat loaf on rolled-out pastry. Moisten edges of pastry with water. Wrap pastry around meat loaf, pinching edges to seal. Turn seam-side down. Preheat oven to 400°F (205°C). Brush pastry with egg yolk. Cut decorative slits in pastry for steam to escape. Bake 20 to 25 minutes in preheated oven until pastry is golden brown. Makes 2 servings.

Quick Corn Dogs

Covering the frankfurters completely with batter keeps the oil from penetrating.

Vegetable oil for frying
4 frankfurters
1/4 cup CORN BREAD MIX, page 23
2 tablespoons all-purpose flour

1/8 teaspoon dry mustard
Pinch paprika
1 egg, slightly beaten
1 tablespoon water

Pour oil 2 to 3 inches deep in a deep-fryer or medium-size heavy saucepan. Dry frankfurters with paper towels; set aside. In a pie plate, combine CORN BREAD MIX, flour, dry mustard and paprika. Stir in egg and water until evenly distributed. Batter will be stiff. Roll frankfurters in batter, covering completely. Use tongs to lower coated frankfurters into hot oil. Turning once, fry until browned, 2 to 3 minutes. Drain on paper towels. Makes 2 servings.

Stuffed Porcupine Peppers

Fill the peppers early in the day, then cover and reheat 20 minutes at 350°F (175°C).

2 large green peppers
1 (8-oz.) can tomato sauce
1/4 cup water
1/4 teaspoon salt
1/8 teaspoon chili powder

1 pkg. MEAT LOAF MIX,
  page 48, thawed
1/2 cup instant rice, uncooked
Cherry tomatoes for garnish, if desired

In a medium saucepan, bring 2 quarts water to a boil. Cut peppers in half lengthwise; remove membranes and seeds. Use tongs to lower peppers into boiling water. Simmer 5 minutes. Remove from boiling water; discard water. Drain peppers cut-side down on paper towels. In a small bowl, combine tomato sauce, water, salt and chili powder; set aside. Preheat oven to 350°F (175°C). Lightly grease a 9-inch square baking dish. In a medium bowl, combine MEAT LOAF MIX and rice. Fill drained peppers with rice mixture. Arrange stuffed peppers in prepared baking dish. Pour tomato sauce mixture over stuffed peppers. Bake 40 minutes in preheated oven until rice is puffed and tender. To serve, arrange stuffed peppers on a small oval platter. Garnish with cherry tomatoes. Makes 2 servings.

How to Make Stuffed Porcupine Peppers

1/Cut peppers in half lengthwise; remove membranes and seeds. Simmer 5 minutes in boiling water.

2/Stuff peppers with meat mixture. Score surface, if desired. Pour sauce over. Bake as directed.

Corn Bread

Spoon unbaked batter over hot CHILI BEANS & WHEAT MIX, page 49. Bake as directed below.

1 egg, slightly beaten
1/2 cup water
2 tablespoons butter, margarine or
  bacon fat, melted

1-1/4 cups CORN BREAD MIX, page 23

Preheat oven to 425°F (220°C). Butter a 5" x 3" loaf pan. In a small bowl, combine egg, water and butter, margarine or bacon fat. Beat with a wire whisk to blend. Stir in CORN BREAD MIX with a fork until just moistened. Batter will be lumpy. Pour into prepared pan. Bake 20 to 25 minutes in preheated oven until browned and a wooden pick inserted in center comes out clean. Makes 2 or 3 servings.

Lime Tarts Supreme

Creamy chiffon filling is topped with a dollop of whipped cream and grated lime peel.

1 pkg. CREAM CHEESE PASTRY
  MIX, page 47, thawed

Lime Filling, see below

Lime Filling:
2 eggs
1/2 cup sugar
1/4 cup lime juice
1 teaspoon grated lime peel

1/4 cup butter or margarine
2 drops green food coloring, if desired
1 cup whipping cream, whipped

Preheat oven to 400°F (205°C). Divide CREAM CHEESE PASTRY MIX into 10 pieces. Shape each piece into a ball. Place each ball in a medium muffin cup. Use your thumbs to press dough over bottom and up side of each cup, keeping dough at an even thickness. Bake in preheated oven 10 minutes or until lightly browned. Cool on a rack. Prepare Lime Filling. Carefully remove cooled tart shells from muffin cups. Spoon filling evenly into shells. Garnish with reserved whipped cream and reserved lime peel from filling. Makes 10 tarts.

Lime Filling:
In a small bowl, beat eggs until light and pale. Beat in sugar, lime juice and half of lime peel until blended. Pour into top of double boiler. Add butter or margarine. Cook and stir over hot water until thickened. Remove from heat. Stir in food coloring, if desired. Refrigerate 1 hour. Reserve 3 tablespoons whipped cream. Fold remaining whipped cream into chilled egg mixture.

Pecan Tarts

Miniature pecan pies are always a welcome treat for family or guests.

1 pkg. CREAM CHEESE PASTRY **MIX, page 47, thawed**	**1-1/2 cups packed brown sugar** **1/8 teaspoon salt**
2 eggs, slightly beaten	**2 teaspoons vanilla extract**
2 tablespoons butter or margarine, melted	**1-1/4 cups chopped pecans**

Divide CREAM CHEESE PASTRY MIX into 10 pieces. Shape each piece into a ball. Place each ball in a medium muffin cup. Use your thumbs to press dough over bottom and up side of each cup, keeping dough at an even thickness; set aside. In a large bowl, combine eggs, butter or margarine, brown sugar, salt and vanilla, beating with a wire whisk until blended. Stir in pecans. Preheat oven to 325°F (165°C). Fill each pastry shell about 3/4 full. Bake 25 minutes in preheated oven until golden brown. Makes 10 tarts.

Chess Tarts

Serve these Southern favorites at a holiday buffet.

1 pkg. CREAM CHEESE PASTRY **MIX, page 47, thawed**	**3 eggs, separated** **3/4 cup raisins**
1/2 cup butter or margarine, softened	**3/4 cup chopped nuts**
1-1/4 cups sugar	**1 teaspoon vanilla extract**

Divide CREAM CHEESE PASTRY MIX into 10 pieces. Shape each piece into a ball. Place each ball in a medium muffin cup. Use your thumbs to press dough over bottom and up side of each cup, keeping dough at an even thickness; set aside. In a large bowl, cream butter or margarine and sugar. Add egg yolks 1 at a time, beating thoroughly after each addition. Stir in raisins, nuts and vanilla. Preheat oven to 400°F (205°C). In a medium bowl, beat egg whites until soft peaks form. Fold into creamed mixture. Fill each pastry shell about 3/4 full with batter. Bake 15 minutes in preheated oven. Reduce temperature to 325°F (165°C). Bake 10 to 15 minutes longer until golden brown. Makes 10 tarts.

Lemon Pound Cake   *Photo on page 12.*

Wrap one of the cakes in heavy-duty foil or moisture-vapor proof paper and freeze it.

2-1/2 cups CRUMB CAKE MIX, page 23	**1 teaspoon grated lemon peel**
1/4 cup sugar	**3 eggs**
1/2 cup milk	**Powdered sugar**
3/4 teaspoon lemon extract	

Generously grease and lightly flour two 7" x 3" loaf pans. In a large bowl, combine CRUMB CAKE MIX, sugar, milk, lemon extract and lemon peel. Beat with electric mixer on medium speed 1 minute. Preheat oven to 375°F (190°C). Scrape batter from side of bowl with a rubber spatula. Beat on high speed 1 minute longer. Add eggs 1 at a time, beating well after each addition until batter is creamy. Pour into prepared pans. Bake 30 to 35 minutes in preheated oven until a wooden pick inserted in center comes out clean. Cool on a rack 10 minutes. Invert onto rack; remove pan. When completely cool, sprinkle with powdered sugar. Makes 2 loaf cakes.

Yellow Crumb Cake

The secret to this moist, tender cake is to beat the batter until creamy.

2 cups CRUMB CAKE MIX, page 23
1/2 cup milk
1/2 teaspoon vanilla extract

2 eggs
Pink Cloud Frosting, see below

Pink Cloud Frosting:
1 egg white, room temperature
1/4 cup sugar
1/3 cup white corn syrup

1/2 teaspoon vanilla extract
2 drops red food coloring

Generously grease and lightly flour an 8-inch, round cake pan or a 6-1/2-inch square baking pan; set aside. Preheat oven to 375°F (190°C). In a large bowl, combine CRUMB CAKE MIX, milk and vanilla. Beat with electric mixer on high speed 1 minute. Scrape batter from side of bowl with a rubber spatula. Beat on high speed 1 minute longer. Add eggs 1 at a time, beating well after each addition until batter is creamy. Pour into prepared pan. Bake 30 to 35 minutes in preheated oven until a wooden pick inserted in center comes out clean. Cool on a rack 10 minutes. Invert onto rack; remove pan. Prepare Pink Cloud Frosting. Frost when cake is completely cool. Makes about 4 servings.

Pink Cloud Frosting:
In a medium bowl, beat egg white with electric mixer until stiff peaks form. Gradually beat in sugar until thick and glossy. Beat in corn syrup, vanilla and food coloring until stiff, 5 to 7 minutes. Makes 1 to 1-1/2 cups.

Chocolate Crumb Cake

For a fudge flavor, add one additional ounce of melted chocolate.

1-3/4 cups CRUMB CAKE MIX, page 23
1/4 cup sugar
1/2 cup milk
1/2 teaspoon vanilla extract
2 (1-oz.) squares unsweetened chocolate,
  melted

2 eggs
Cream Cheese Frosting from
  Carrot Snack Cake, page 113

Generously grease and lightly flour an 8-inch, round cake pan or a 6-1/2-inch square baking pan; set aside. In a large bowl, combine CRUMB CAKE MIX, sugar, milk and vanilla. Beat with electric mixer on high speed 1 minute. Stir in melted chocolate until blended. Preheat oven to 375°F (190°C). Scrape batter from side of bowl with a rubber spatula. Beat on high speed 1 minute longer. Add eggs 1 at a time, beating well after each addition until batter is creamy. Pour into prepared pan. Bake 30 to 35 minutes in preheated oven until a wooden pick inserted in center comes out clean. Cool on a rack 10 minutes. Invert onto rack; remove pan. When completely cool, frost with Cream Cheese Frosting. Makes 4 servings.

Almond Kringle

The filling puffs up and makes a soft, flaky layer.

**1 pkg. CREAM CHEESE PASTRY
  MIX, page 47, thawed
1/2 cup water
1/4 cup butter or margarine
1/2 cup all-purpose flour**

**2 eggs
1/4 teaspoon almond extract
Kringle Icing, see below
1/4 cup sliced almonds**

Kringle Icing:
**1/2 cup powdered sugar
1-1/2 teaspoons cream or milk**

**2 teaspoons butter or margarine
1/2 teaspoon almond extract**

Roll out CREAM CHEESE PASTRY MIX into a 14'' x 4'' rectangle. Place rolled-out dough on a large baking sheet. Crimp and shape sides of dough to make a raised edge. Preheat oven to 350°F (175°C). In a small saucepan, combine water and butter or margarine. Bring to a boil over medium-high heat. Add flour all at once, stirring vigorously until mixture forms a ball and leaves side of pan. Remove from heat. Add eggs 1 at a time, beating well after each addition. Beat in almond extract. Spread mixture over pastry. Bake 40 to 45 minutes in preheated oven until golden brown. Cool on a rack 5 minutes. Prepare Kringle Icing. Spread over baked filling. Sprinkle with sliced almonds. To serve, cut in 1-1/2-inch diagonal slices. Makes about 6 servings.

Kringle Icing:
In a small bowl, combine all ingredients, beating until smooth.

How to Make Almond Kringle

1/Roll out dough on a large baking sheet. Crimp and shape sides to make raised edge.

2/Spread frosting over baked filling. With a sharp knife, cut Kringle diagonally.

Light & Tender Biscuits

The convenience of mixes is apparent when biscuits are this easy to make.

1-1/2 cups QUICK MIX, page 21
1/3 cup milk or water

In a medium bowl, combine QUICK MIX and milk or water. Stir with a fork to blend. Let dough rest 5 minutes. Preheat oven to 450°F (230°C). On a lightly floured board, knead dough about 15 times. Roll out 1/2 inch thick. Cut with a biscuit cutter or top of a large thin drinking glass. Place cut biscuits about 2 inches apart on an ungreased baking sheet. Bake 10 to 12 minutes in preheated oven until golden brown. Makes 6 large biscuits.

Variation

Apple Cobbler: Place 2 cups sliced apples in a 6-1/2-inch square baking pan. Sprinkle with 1 tablespoon lemon juice. Combine 3 tablespoons sugar and 1/2 teaspoon cinnamon. Sprinkle over apples. Stir 2 tablespoons sugar into QUICK MIX. Prepare Light & Tender Biscuit dough as directed above. Drop dough by spoonfuls over fruit. Bake at 325°F (165°C) 35 to 40 minutes until dough is browned and fruit is tender. Makes 2 to 4 servings.

Fruit Muffins

Substitute chopped apple or fresh blueberries for the raisins or dates.

1 egg, beaten
1/2 cup milk or water
2 tablespoons sugar

1-1/4 cups QUICK MIX, page 21
1/2 cup raisins or dates
1/2 cup chopped nuts

Preheat oven to 425°F (220°C). Generously grease 6 large muffin cups. In a small bowl, combine egg and milk or water. In a second small bowl, stir sugar into QUICK MIX. Add egg mixture all at once, stirring until just moistened. Stir in raisins or dates and nuts. Fill each prepared muffin cup 2/3 full with batter. Bake 15 to 20 minutes in preheated oven until golden brown and a wooden pick inserted in center comes out dry. Makes 6 large muffins.

Quick Pancakes

Serve these tender pancakes with syrup from Waffles with Pioneer Syrup, page 142.

1 egg, beaten
3/4 cup milk or water

1-1/4 cups QUICK MIX, page 21
1-1/2 teaspoons sugar

In a small bowl, combine egg and milk or water. In another small bowl, combine QUICK MIX and sugar. Add egg mixture all at once, stirring with a wire whisk to blend. Let stand 3 to 5 minutes. Preheat griddle according to manufacturer's directions. Lightly oil hot griddle. Pour about 1/3 cup batter onto hot griddle to make 1 pancake. Cook until edge becomes dry and bubbles form. Turn with a wide spatula. Cook 35 to 45 seconds until browned. Repeat with remaining batter. Makes about six 4-inch pancakes.

High Health

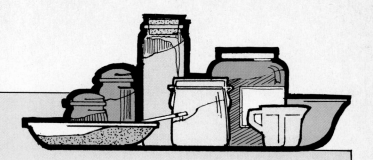

Homemade mixes in this section help you increase the nutritional level of the foods you eat and minimize time spent preparing them. We did not try to eliminate all white flour or sugar. You are aware of what you consume and can decide what you want to change. Analyze each recipe you use to determine if ingredients can be added, altered or changed to increase nutritional value without sacrificing taste or quality.

If your family is not used to the flavor of whole-wheat flour, try introducing it in small amounts. They may prefer half all-purpose or unbleached flour and half whole-wheat flour. When substituting one for the other, 1 cup whole-wheat flour minus 2 tablespoons equals 1 cup all-purpose or unbleached flour. Whole-wheat flour is heavier than all-purpose flour, so increase the leavening agent when you adapt a recipe. As a general rule, increase baking powder and baking soda by 1/3 and double the yeast. Store whole-wheat flour in the refrigerator or freezer to retain freshness and retard loss of nutrients. Use it soon after it is ground.

Substitute raw sugar, granulated sugar and brown sugar in equal proportions. If you substitute 1 cup honey or corn syrup for 1 cup sugar, reduce liquid in the recipe by 1/4 cup and add 1/4 teaspoon baking soda unless baking soda is already an ingredient in the recipe. Baking soda neutralizes the acidity of honey.

Commercial seasoning mixes contain a lot of salt. If you are on a salt-restricted diet you can reduce the salt content of a mix you make yourself or replace it with a salt substitute.

For a nutritionally balanced diet, start with a good breakfast. WHEAT & BRAN MUFFIN MIX, page 35, provides exceptional taste and true convenience. When children won't take time for breakfast, give them a glass of juice and a plastic bag of TRAIL MIX, page 26, and send them off to school or to play. They won't be able to resist this snack.

Nutri-Nut Breakfast Bars

These bars give you nearly complete nutrition. Just add some fruit.

1-1/2 cups NUTRI-NUT CEREAL MIX,
  page 25
3 tablespoons instant
  nonfat milk powder
1/8 teaspoon salt
1/4 teaspoon ground cinnamon

1/4 cup raisins
1 tablespoon vegetable oil
2 tablespoons honey
1 teaspoon vanilla extract
1/3 cup peanut butter
1 egg, slightly beaten

Preheat oven to 250°F (120°C). Grease and flour an 8-inch square baking pan; set aside. In a medium bowl, combine NUTRI-NUT CEREAL MIX, milk powder, salt, cinnamon and raisins. In a small bowl, combine oil, honey, vanilla, peanut butter and egg, stirring with a wire whisk to blend. Stir egg mixture into raisin mixture. Press into prepared baking pan. Bake 25 minutes in preheated oven until browned. Cool on a rack 10 minutes. Cut in 2-inch squares. Makes about 16 servings.

Swiss Porridge

Try this different breakfast treat for dessert.

1 pt. fresh strawberries
1 (20-oz.) can crushed pineapple
1 cup SPICED OATMEAL MIX,
   page 25
2 bananas, sliced
1/3 cup finely chopped nuts

1 tablespoon lemon juice
Grated peel of 1 lemon
   (about 1-1/2 teaspoons)
1 cup whipping cream
1 (8-oz.) carton plain yogurt

Reserve 8 whole strawberries. Slice remaining strawberries; set aside. Drain pineapple, reserving juice. In a small bowl, combine SPICED OATMEAL MIX and pineapple juice; set aside. In a medium bowl, combine drained pineapple, sliced strawberries, bananas and nuts. Sprinkle with lemon juice and lemon peel. Toss lightly with 2 forks. In a large bowl, whip cream until stiff peaks form. Reserve 1 cup whipped cream. Fold yogurt into remaining whipped cream. Fold fruit mixture into yogurt mixture. Gently stir in oatmeal mixture. Refrigerate at least 1 hour. Spoon porridge evenly into 8 parfait glasses or custard cups. Garnish each serving with 2 tablespoons reserved whipped cream and 1 whole strawberry. Makes 8 servings.

Delicious Wheat Pancakes

Add sliced bananas or grated apples to the batter.

1 egg, slightly beaten
1-1/3 cups water

2 cups HONEY & WHEAT MIX,
   page 33

In a medium bowl, combine egg and water, beating with a wire whisk to blend. Stir in HONEY & WHEAT MIX until blended. Let stand 2 minutes. Preheat griddle according to manufacturer's instructions. Lightly oil griddle. Stir in more water if a thinner batter is desired. Pour about 1/3 cup batter onto hot griddle to make 1 pancake. Cook until edge becomes dry and bubbles form. Turn with a wide spatula. Cook 35 to 45 seconds longer until browned on both sides. Repeat with remaining batter. Makes about ten 4-inch pancakes.

Spicy Oatmeal Pancakes

Pancakes made with this thin batter have a delightfully spicy flavor.

2 cups SPICED OATMEAL MIX,
   page 25
2 cups hot milk
1/2 cup butter or margarine, melted

2 eggs, slightly beaten
1/2 cup unbleached flour or
   all-purpose flour
2 teaspoons baking powder

In a medium bowl, combine SPICED OATMEAL MIX, hot milk and butter or margarine, stirring with a wire whisk to blend. Set aside to cool. Beat in eggs 1 at a time until blended. Stir in flour and baking powder until just blended. Let stand 2 minutes. Preheat griddle according to manufacturer's instructions. Lightly oil griddle. Pour about 1/3 cup batter onto hot griddle to make 1 pancake. Cook until edge becomes dry and bubbles form. Turn with a wide spatula. Cook 35 to 45 seconds longer until browned on both sides. Repeat with remaining batter. Makes about eighteen 3-inch pancakes.

Waffles with Pioneer Syrup

For a milder flavored syrup, use all granulated sugar.

3 eggs, separated
2 cups buttermilk
1/4 cup butter or margarine, melted
3 cups HONEY & WHEAT MIX,
    page 33

3/4 teaspoon baking soda
Pioneer Syrup, see below

Pioneer Syrup:
1 cup water
3/4 cup granulated sugar

3/4 cup packed brown sugar
3/4 teaspoon maple flavoring

Preheat waffle iron. In a medium bowl, combine egg yolks, buttermilk and butter or margarine, beating with a wire whisk to blend. In a large bowl, combine HONEY & WHEAT MIX and baking soda. Stir into buttermilk mixture until just moistened. Batter will be lumpy. Beat egg whites until stiff but not dry. Fold into batter. Bake in waffle iron according to manufacturer's instructions. Serve hot with Pioneer Syrup. Makes 4 large waffles.

Pioneer Syrup:
In a small saucepan, bring water to a boil over medium-high heat. Gradually stir in granulated sugar and brown sugar until dissolved. Stir in maple flavoring. Serve over hot waffles. Refrigerate remaining syrup. Makes about 2 cups.

Spiced Oatmeal

When serving two people, double the proportions.

1/2 cup water
1/2 cup SPICED OATMEAL MIX,
    page 25

Milk

In a small saucepan, bring water to a boil. Stir in SPICED OATMEAL MIX. Stirring occasionally, simmer over medium-low heat 1 to 2 minutes. Serve with milk. Makes 1 serving.

Breakfast Parfait

NUTRI-NUT CEREAL MIX served with hot or cold milk makes a quick, nutritious breakfast.

1 (8-oz.) carton plain yogurt
1 tablespoon lemon juice
2 teaspoons honey

3/4 cup NUTRI-NUT CEREAL MIX,
    page 25
1 cup sliced strawberries or bananas

In a small bowl, combine yogurt, lemon juice and honey, stirring to blend. In each of 2 parfait glasses, layer 3 tablespoons NUTRI-NUT CEREAL MIX, 1/4 cup yogurt mixture and 1/4 cup sliced stawberries or bananas. Repeat layers. Makes 2 servings.

Bran-Ana Muffins

To make bran muffins, omit the banana and add one egg.

1 egg, slightly beaten	**3/4 cup water**
1 cup mashed bananas	**3 cups MOLASSES &**
1/4 cup vegetable oil	**BRAN MUFFIN MIX, page 35**

Grease 12 large muffin cups. In a medium bowl, combine egg, mashed bananas, oil and water, beating with a wire whisk to blend. Add MOLASSES & BRAN MUFFIN MIX all at once, stirring until just moistened. Batter will be lumpy. Let stand 10 minutes to soften bran. Preheat oven to 400°F (205°C). Fill each prepared muffin cup 2/3 full with batter. Bake 15 to 20 minutes in preheated oven until golden brown and a wooden pick inserted in center comes out dry. Makes 12 large muffins.

Honey & Wheat Muffins

Naturally sweet and tender, these muffins will add extra nutrition to a meal.

3 cups HONEY & WHEAT MIX, page 33	**1 egg, slightly beaten**
2 tablespoons packed brown sugar	**1-1/3 cups water**

Preheat oven to 400°F (205°C). Generously grease 12 large muffin cups. In a large bowl, combine HONEY & WHEAT MIX and brown sugar. In a small bowl, combine egg and water, beating with a wire whisk to blend. Add egg mixture all at once to brown sugar mixture, stirring until just moistened. Batter will be lumpy. Fill each prepared muffin cup 2/3 full with batter. Bake 15 to 20 minutes in preheated oven until golden brown and a wooden pick inserted in center comes out dry. Makes 12 large muffins.

Buttermilk Biscuits

Substitute these tender biscuits for the Rice Ring in Ring-Around-the-Tuna, page 81.

2 cups HONEY & WHEAT MIX, page 33	**1/2 cup buttermilk, milk or water**

Pour HONEY & WHEAT MIX into a medium bowl. Add buttermilk, milk or water all at once. Stir with a fork until dough follows fork around bowl. Preheat oven to 450°F ((230°C). Turn out dough on a lightly floured surface. Knead 10 to 12 times. Roll out to 1/2 inch thick. Use a 2-inch biscuit cutter to cut rolled-out dough. Arrange dough circles on an ungreased baking sheet. Bake 10 to 12 minutes in preheated oven until lightly browned. Makes about 9 biscuits.

Chili Mexicano

Heat individual servings in your microwave oven.

**3 pkgs. CHILI BEANS &
 WHEAT MIX, page 49, thawed**

1 (10-oz.) pkg. corn chips
3/4 cup shredded Cheddar cheese (3 oz.)

In a medium saucepan, heat CHILI BEANS & WHEAT MIX. In each of 4 soup bowls, layer about 1/3 cup corn chips, 3 tablespoons shredded cheese and 1-1/4 to 1-1/2 cups hot chili. Serve immediately. Makes 4 servings.

Chili Tostadas

Tostada shells are flat corn tortillas cooked crisp.

**1 pkg. CHILI BEANS &
 WHEAT MIX, page 49, thawed**
6 tostada shells

1/2 head lettuce, shredded
3 cups shredded Cheddar cheese (12 oz.)
1 large tomato, chopped

In a medium bowl, partially crush CHILI BEANS & WHEAT MIX with a potato masher or a fork. In a medium saucepan, simmer partially crushed mix over medium heat about 5 minutes. Spread evenly over tostada shells. Top evenly with lettuce, shredded cheese and chopped tomato. Makes 6 servings.

Variations

Substitute taco shells for tostada shells.

Omit tostada shells. Spoon hot CHILI BEANS & WHEAT MIX on hot dogs in buns. Top with shredded lettuce and shredded cheese, if desired.

Substitute 3 cut French rolls for tostada shells. Sprinkle each half roll with grated cheese. Broil to melt cheese. Top with hot CHILI BEANS & WHEAT MIX, lettuce and chopped tomato.

Substitute 3 split English muffins for tostada shells and 6 slices Swiss cheese for the Cheddar cheese. Top each half muffin with 1 slice Swiss cheese. Broil to melt cheese. Top with hot CHILI BEANS & WHEAT MIX, shredded lettuce and chopped tomato.

Mexican Pinwheels

Serve these savory pinwheel appetizers with crisp carrot curls and celery fans.

**2 cups CHILI BEANS &
 WHEAT MIX, page 49, thawed**

4 (10-inch) whole-wheat flour tortillas
1 cup shredded Cheddar cheese (4 oz.)

In a blender, process CHILI BEANS & WHEAT MIX on high speed 2 minutes until smooth. Arrange tortillas on a large baking sheet. Spread about 1/2 cup pureed mix on each tortilla. Sprinkle evenly with shredded cheese. Preheat broiler, if necessary. Broil 2 inches below heating element until cheese is melted and chili is hot. Tortilla will be soft. Roll up jelly-roll fashion. Cut in 1/2-inch slices. Arrange on a small platter. Serve hot. Makes about 30 appetizers.

Chicken with Fruit Stuffing

Also use this flavorful stuffing in squab, duck or turkey.

1 medium orange	**2 tablespoons butter or margarine**
1 small apple	**1/2 cup chopped celery**
1 cup GRANOLA MIX, page 24	**1/4 cup chopped onion**
1-1/4 cups cooked long-grain rice	**2 (3-lb.) whole broiler fryers**
1/2 teaspoon salt	**Vegetable oil**
1/4 teaspoon ground cinnamon	**Parsley sprigs for garnish**

Peel and section orange, removing section membranes. Cut each orange section into 3 pieces. Peel, core and chop apple. In a large bowl, combine orange pieces, chopped apple, GRANOLA MIX, cooked rice, salt and cinnamon. In a small skillet, melt butter or margarine. Add celery and onion; sauté until crisp-tender. Add to fruit mixture, tossing lightly with 2 forks. Preheat oven to 375°F (190°C). Spoon stuffing evenly into body cavities of chickens. Moisten your hands with oil. Rub oil evenly over chickens. Place on broiler rack over broiler pan. Cover chickens loosely with foil. Bake 1-1/2 hours in preheated oven. Remove foil. Bake 30 minutes longer until chickens are lightly browned and tender. To serve, arrange baked chickens side-by-side on a large platter. Garnish with parsley sprigs. Makes 6 to 8 servings.

How to Section Oranges

1/Use a thin-blade knife to remove peel and white membrane from orange.

2/To section orange, cut on both sides of membrane sections. Remove fruit.

Quick Baked Chimichangas

Baked chimichangas have fewer calories than the traditionally deep-fried ones.

**2 pkgs. CHILI BEANS &
  WHEAT MIX, page 49, thawed**
**3 tablespoons diced or
  chopped green chilies**
8 (10-inch) whole-wheat flour tortillas
1/4 cup butter or margarine, melted

4 cups shredded lettuce
1 (7-oz.) can mild green chili salsa
1 cup dairy sour cream for garnish
**1 avocado, mashed, or
  1 (7-3/4-oz.) pkg. guacamole dip**
8 ripe olives for garnish

Lightly grease a large baking sheet; set aside. In a blender, combine CHILI BEANS & WHEAT MIX and green chilies. Process on high speed 2 minutes until pureed. Preheat oven to 350°F (175°C). Spoon about 1/2 cup mixture on center of each tortilla. Fold edge closest to you over filling. Fold both sides toward center; roll tortilla toward free edge. Arrange on prepared baking sheet, seam-side down. Brush each with melted butter or margarine. Bake about 20 minutes in preheated oven until golden brown and slightly crisp. Serve on shredded lettuce. Top evenly with green chili salsa. Garnish each with 2 tablespoons sour cream, 1 tablespoon mashed avocado or guacamole dip and 1 ripe olive. Makes 8 servings.

Variation

Omit baking. Substitute oil for frying for melted butter or margarine. Pour oil 2 inches deep in a medium saucepan. Heat to 375°F (190°C). At this temperature a 1-inch cube of bread will turn golden brown in 40 seconds. Use tongs to lower rolled, filled tortillas into hot oil 1 at a time. Fry until golden brown and crisp. Drain on paper towels. Serve as directed above.

Irresistible Apples

The stuffing in these apples makes them perfect to pack in lunches or take on hikes.

1/4 cup peanut butter
1/4 cup instant nonfat milk powder
1/4 cup honey
**1/4 cup NUTRI-NUT CEREAL MIX,
  page 25**

1/4 cup raisins
6 large apples

In a medium bowl, combine peanut butter, milk powder, honey, NUTRI-NUT CEREAL MIX and raisins. Stir with a fork to blend. Rinse and core apples. Spoon filling evenly into center of each apple. Wrap each apple in plastic wrap. Refrigerate at least 1 hour. Makes 6 servings.

Good-for-You Gems

Use creamy or chunk-style peanut butter.

1/2 cup instant nonfat milk powder
1/2 cup honey
1/2 cup peanut butter

1-1/2 cups GRANOLA MIX, page 24,
or NUTRI-NUT CEREAL MIX,
page 25

In a medium bowl, combine milk powder, honey, peanut butter and 3/4 cup GRANOLA MIX or NUTRI-NUT CEREAL MIX. Stir with a wooden spoon to blend. Dampen your hands slightly. Knead mixture 5 or 6 times. Add more milk powder if mixture is quite sticky. Shape into balls about the size of large olives or into other shapes, if desired. Roll balls in remaining 3/4 cup GRANOLA MIX or NUTRI-NUT CEREAL MIX. Makes about thirty 3/4-inch balls.

How to Make Good-for-You Gems

1/Combine milk powder, honey, peanut butter and 3/4 cup mix.

2/Shape into balls, logs or other shapes. Roll in remaining mix.

Granola Fruit Crisp

You'll need about six cups of sliced or chopped fruit.

Granola Topping, see below
3 tablespoons packed brown sugar
3 tablespoons whole-wheat flour

1 teaspoon ground cinnamon
9 apples, peaches or pears
2 tablespoons lemon juice

Granola Topping:
2 cups GRANOLA MIX, page 24
1 cup whole-wheat flour

1/2 cup butter or margarine, melted

Butter a 13" x 9" baking pan; set aside. Prepare Granola Topping; set aside. Preheat oven to 375°F (190°C). In a medium bowl, combine brown sugar, whole-wheat flour and cinnamon; set aside. Peel and slice or chop fruit. Sprinkle with lemon juice. Turn into flour mixture, stirring until evenly coated. Spoon into prepared baking pan. Sprinkle topping over fruit. Bake 25 to 30 minutes in preheated oven until topping is browned and fruit is tender. Makes 8 to 10 servings.

Granola Topping:
In a medium bowl, combine GRANOLA MIX and whole-wheat flour. Pour melted butter or margarine over mixture, stirring to blend.

Granola Energy Bars

Serve these high-energy trail bars as a snack anytime of the day.

1/2 cup packed dark brown sugar
1/2 cup light corn syrup
1/2 cup peanut butter

3-1/2 cups GRANOLA MIX, page 24
1/2 cup Spanish peanuts

Butter a 9-inch square baking pan; set aside. In a large saucepan, combine brown sugar and corn syrup. Cook and stir over medium heat until mixture comes to a boil. Remove from heat. Stir in peanut butter until blended. Stir in GRANOLA MIX and Spanish peanuts until coated. Press into prepared pan. Cool to room temperature. Cut into 3" x 1" rectangles. Makes 27 bars.

Children's Mixes

Children like to be creative. Let your children have the experience of making the mixes and recipes in this section, and then share in the joy of eating their creations. They may need some supervision the first time, but later, let them follow the instructions on their own. Our children have made these mixes for several years.

Most children will have no difficulty making these small-quantity recipes. Usually, they simply add water. The cakes and cookies can be baked in a child's play oven or in a regular oven.

Small mixing equipment that fits your children's hands will make it easier for them to work. Remove the fear of breaking something by giving them plastic or metal bowls to mix in. As children get older, introduce them to other mixes in the book. Soon you will find yourselves with confident helpers in the kitchen.

Children's Lemon Cake Mix

For a white cake mix, omit the lemon flavoring.

1 cup sugar
1-1/2 cups all-purpose flour
1 teaspoon baking soda
1/2 teaspoon salt

1 teaspoon Burst-O-Lemon or
    unsweetened lemon-flavored drink powder
1/3 cup vegetable shortening

In a medium bowl, combine sugar, flour, baking soda, salt and Burst-O-Lemon or lemon-flavored drink powder. Stir with a wire whisk until blended. With a pastry blender, cut in shortening until evenly distributed and mixture resembles cornmeal. Spoon about 1/3-cup into each of 10 small containers with tight-fitting lids. Seal containers. Label with date and contents. Store in a cool dry place. Use within 12 weeks. Makes 10 packages CHILDREN'S LEMON CAKE MIX.

Little Lemon Cake

1 pkg. CHILDREN'S LEMON CAKE
    MIX, see above
4 teaspoons water

Childrens White Frosting, page 152,
    if desired

Preheat Mom's oven to 375°F (190°C). If using a child's play oven, follow manufacturer's directions for baking cakes. Grease and flour a 4-inch, round miniature cake pan. In a small bowl, combine CHILDREN'S LEMON CAKE MIX and water. Stir with a fork or spoon until blended and smooth. Pour mixture into prepared pan. Bake 12 to 13 minutes in Mom's preheated oven or as directed for childs play oven. Remove from oven. Cool on a rack 5 minutes. Invert cake and pan onto a small plate; remove pan. When cool, frost with Children's White Frosting, if desired. Makes 2 servings.

Children's Chocolate Cake Mix

Just add water to make a cake from this mix.

1 cup sugar
3 tablespoons unsweetened cocoa powder
1-1/2 cups all-purpose flour

1 teaspoon baking soda
1/2 teaspoon salt
1/3 cup vegetable shortening

In a medium bowl, combine sugar, cocoa powder, flour, baking soda and salt. Stir with a wire whisk until blended. With a pastry blender, cut in shortening until evenly distributed and mixture resembles cornmeal. Spoon about 1/3 cup into each of 11 small containers with tight-fitting lids. Seal containers. Label with date and contents. Store in a cool dry place. Use within 12 weeks. Makes 11 packages CHILDREN'S CHOCOLATE CAKE MIX.

Little Chocolate Cake

1 pkg. CHILDREN'S CHOCOLATE
  CAKE MIX, see above
4 teaspoons water

Children's Chocolate Frosting, page 152,
  if desired

Preheat Mom's oven to 375°F (190°C). If using a child's play oven, follow manufacturer's directions for baking cakes. Grease and flour a 4-inch, round miniature cake pan. In a small bowl, combine CHILDREN'S CHOCOLATE CAKE MIX and water. Stir with a fork or spoon until blended and smooth. Pour mixture into prepared pan. Bake 12 to 13 minutes in Mom's preheated oven or as directed for child's play oven. Remove from oven; cool on a rack 5 minutes. Invert cake and pan onto a small plate; remove pan. When cool, frost with Children's Chocolate Frosting, if desired. Makes 2 servings.

Children's Cookie Mix

Packed brown sugar *means you press it down into the cup to measure it.*

1-1/2 cups quick-cooking rolled oats
3/4 cup all-purpose flour
1/4 teaspoon baking soda

3/4 cup packed brown sugar
1/2 cup vegetable shortening

In a medium bowl, combine oats, flour, baking soda and brown sugar. Stir to blend. Cut in shortening with a pastry blender until mixture resembles cornmeal. Spoon about 1/2 cup each into 8 small containers with tight-fitting lids. Seal containers. Label with date and contents. Store in a cool dry place. Use within 10 to 12 weeks. Makes 8 packages CHILDREN'S COOKIE MIX.

Raisin-Chip Cookies

1/2 cup CHILDREN'S COOKIE MIX,
  see above
2 teaspoons water

1 tablespoon raisins
1 tablespoon small chocolate pieces
Sugar

Preheat Mom's oven to 350°F (175°C). If using a child's play oven, follow manufacturer's directions for baking cookies. In a small bowl, combine CHILDREN'S COOKIE MIX, water, raisins and chocolate pieces. Stir with a spoon until mixture holds together in one big ball. Shape 1 teaspoon of dough at a time into a ball. Arrange on an ungreased cookie sheet. Butter bottom of a small drinking glass. Dip buttered glass bottom in sugar. Flatten each ball by pressing with sugar-coated glass. Bake 10 to 12 minutes in Mom's preheated oven or as directed for child's play oven. Remove from oven. Cool on a rack. Makes about 9 cookies.

How to Make Raisin-Chip Cookies

1/Shape dough into balls. Place balls on an ungreased baking sheet.

2/Press dough with bottom of buttered and sugar-coated drinking glass.

Children's White Frosting Mix

Spread this smooth frosting on cookies, graham crackers or on a cake.

2 cups powdered sugar, sifted
3 tablespoons instant
  nonfat milk powder

6 tablespoons vegetable shortening

In a medium bowl, combine powdered sugar and milk powder. Stir with a wire whisk to blend. With pastry blender, cut in shortening. Spoon about 1/3 cup into each of 8 small containers with tight-fitting lids. Seal containers. Label with date and contents. Store in a cool dry place. Use within 12 weeks. Makes 8 packages CHILDREN'S WHITE FROSTING MIX.

Children's White Frosting

1 pkg. CHILDREN'S WHITE
  FROSTING MIX, see above

3/4 teaspoon water

In a small bowl, combine CHILDREN'S WHITE FROSTING MIX and water, stirring with a spoon until smooth. Makes about 1/4 cup.

Children's Chocolate Frosting Mix

Sift the cocoa powder if it has lumps in it.

2 cups powdered sugar, sifted
3 tablespoons instant
  nonfat milk powder

1/2 cup unsweetened cocoa powder
6 tablespoons vegetable shortening

In a medium bowl, combine powdered sugar, milk powder and cocoa powder. With a pastry blender, cut in shortening. Spoon about 1/3 cup into each of 9 small containers with tight-fitting lids. Seal containers. Label with date and contents. Store in a cool dry place. Use within 12 weeks. Makes 9 packages CHILDREN'S CHOCOLATE FROSTING MIX.

Children's Chocolate Frosting

1 pkg. CHILDREN'S CHOCOLATE
  FROSTING MIX, see above

3/4 teaspoon water

In a small bowl, combine CHILDREN'S CHOCOLATE FROSTING MIX and water, stirring with a spoon until smooth. Makes about 1/4 cup.

Index

Equivalency Chart

Food Item	Market Unit	Household measurement
Baking powder	14 oz.	1-3/4 cups
Baking soda	1 lb.	2-1/3 cups
Buttermilk powder	1 lb.	5 cups
Cereal, cold flaked	15 oz.	about 11 cups
Cocoa powder, unsweetened	8 oz.	2 cups
Cornstarch	1 lb.	3-1/2 cups
Cream of Tartar	1-3/4 oz.	5-1/2 tablespoons
Flour		
All-purpose	5 lbs.	about 20 cups
Instant	13.5 oz.	about 3 cups
Whole-wheat	5 lbs.	about 18-1/3 cups
Gelatin		
Unflavored	1 oz.	1/4 cup
Flavored	3 oz.	7 tablespoons
Graham crackers	1 lb.	about 4 cups crumbs
Herb leaves, chopped fresh	2 teaspoons	1/4 teaspoon dried
Lemon juice	1 lemon	3 to 4 tablespoons
Lemon peel, grated	1 lemon	about 1-1/2 teaspoons
Milk, instant nonfat powder	1 lb.	about 6 cups
Oats, rolled	18 oz.	about 6 cups
Onion, chopped fresh	1/4 cup	1 tablespoon dried
Orange juice	1 orange	6 to 8 tablespoons
Orange peel	1 orange	about 1 tablespoon
Sugar		
Brown	1 lb.	2-1/4 cups
Granulated	5 lbs.	about 15 cups
Powdered, unsifted	1 lb.	about 4 cups
Yeast		
Active dry	1/4 oz.	1 tablespoon
Compressed	0.60 oz.	4 teaspoons

Basic measurements:
    1/4 cup = 4 tablespoons = 12 teaspoons
    1 cup = 16 tablespoons = 48 teaspoons
    1 tablespoon = 3 teaspoons

Mix name and page

from

MORE MAKE-A-MIX COOKERY

by Eliason, Harward & Westover

Published by **HPBooks**

Date: Use by _____

Recipe pages _____ _____

_____ _____

_____ _____

Mix name and page

from

MORE MAKE-A-MIX COOKERY

by Eliason, Harward & Westover

Published by **HPBooks**

Date: Use by _____

Recipe pages _____ _____

_____ _____

_____ _____

Mix name and page

from

MORE MAKE-A-MIX COOKERY

by Eliason, Harward & Westover

Published by **HPBooks**

Date: Use by _____

Recipe pages _____ _____

_____ _____

_____ _____

Mix name and page

from

MORE MAKE-A-MIX COOKERY

by Eliason, Harward & Westover

Published by **HPBooks**

Date: Use by _____

Recipe pages _____ _____

_____ _____

_____ _____

Mix name and page

from

MORE MAKE-A-MIX COOKERY

by Eliason, Harward & Westover

Published by **HPBooks**

Date: Use by _____

Recipe pages _____ _____

_____ _____

_____ _____

Mix name and page

from

MORE MAKE-A-MIX COOKERY

by Eliason, Harward & Westover

Published by **HPBooks**

Date: Use by _____

Recipe pages _____ _____

_____ _____

_____ _____

Metric Chart

Comparison to Metric Measure

When You Know	Symbol	Multiply By	To Find	Symbol
teaspoons	tsp	5.0	milliliters	ml
tablespoons	tbsp	15.0	milliliters	ml
fluid ounces	fl. oz.	30.0	milliliters	ml
cups	c	0.24	liters	l
pints	pt.	0.47	liters	l
quarts	qt.	0.95	liters	l
ounces	oz.	28.0	grams	g
pounds	lb.	0.45	kilograms	kg
Fahrenheit	F	5/9 (after subtracting 32)	Celsius	C

Liquid Measure to Milliliters

1/4 teaspoon	=	1.25 milliliters
1/2 teaspoon	=	2.5 milliliters
3/4 teaspoon	=	3.75 milliliters
1 teaspoon	=	5.0 milliliters
1-1/4 teaspoons	=	6.25 milliliters
1-1/2 teaspoons	=	7.5 milliliters
1-3/4 teaspoons	=	8.75 milliliters
2 teaspoons	=	10.0 milliliters
1 tablespoon	=	15.0 milliliters
2 tablespoons	=	30.0 milliliters

Liquid Measure to Liters

1/4 cup	=	0.06 liters
1/2 cup	=	0.12 liters
3/4 cup	=	0.18 liters
1 cup	=	0.24 liters
1-1/4 cups	=	0.3 liters
1-1/2 cups	=	0.36 liters
2 cups	=	0.48 liters
2-1/2 cups	=	0.6 liters
3 cups	=	0.72 liters
3-1/2 cups	=	0.84 liters
4 cups	=	0.96 liters
4-1/2 cups	=	1.08 liters
5 cups	=	1.2 liters
5-1/2 cups	=	1.32 liters

Fahrenheit to Celsius

F	C
200—205	95
220—225	105
245—250	120
275	135
300—305	150
325—330	165
345—350	175
370—375	190
400—405	205
425—430	220
445—450	230
470—475	245
500	260